Marc

Echoes and Reflections
of a
lost Lakeland community

Shap Local History Society

For John Graham, with grateful thanks

John and Joyce Graham in 1995
with the clock presented to
Miss Forster on her retirement as
teacher at Mardale School

Front cover: The head of Mardale in the 1930s merges with the same view in 2010, inset Joyce Bell, with father Maurice and Ronnie Scott the postman. Background map reproduced with the permission of Alan Godfrey Maps.

Back cover: Draw Down Tower, March 2010

Published in 2011 by Shap Local History Society in association with David Grayling Publishing.

ISBN 978-0-906839-06-5

Typesetting and cover design by Indent Ltd, Kendal

Printed by Cerberus Printing, Kirkby Stephen

Contents

Acknowledgements

Shap Local History Society is very grateful to everyone who has helped in the production of this book. In no particular order, but all very important, we would like to thank the following:

John Graham for allowing us full access to his Mardale archive, and for his support and enthusiasm

Lowther Estates for permission to use material from the Lowther Archive at Carlisle Record Office

Friends of the Lake District for permission to use extracts from the Reverend Terry's scrap book

Penrith Museum for permission to reproduce *The Height of Ambition* and *The Downfall of Pride* by Jacob Thompson

Indent Limited for cover design and typesetting

David Grayling

B+J Imaging for help with the black and white photos

John Innerdale for the colour map of Haweswater and Mardale

Bryan Lindley, Patrick Neaves, Ted Relph and Janet Wood for reading and commenting on the first draft

Hannah Amos for proof reading the final draft

Kendal and Carlisle Record Offices

Heritage Lottery Fund

Natural England

Royal Commission on the Historical Monuments of England for permission to reproduce photographs in Chapter 4 from the RCHME survey of England 1935

Descendants of the Baily family for permission to include material from the family archive

Michael and Margaret Green for information on the Green family in Chapter 9

Cynthia Holme and Derek Ellwood for donations towards publication costs

Eric Skipsey for help with geological information.

Colour Plates

Foreword

Some years ago I made a film for the BBC called The King of Mardale. It was not a happy experience. Shortly after the film was shot the director skipped the country with officers of HM Revenue and Customs in hot pursuit. A rough cut of the film was discovered in a drawer of his desk, filed between a half-eaten cheese sandwich and the disputed tax returns. The project was then taken up by a film editor who was monstrously talented and bone idle in equal measure. On the day we were to do the final sound dub in London I found him in the breakfast dining room of the Great Northern Hotel at Kings Cross still trying to complete the dubbing charts, the maze of multi-coloured lines that tell the sound mixer which audio tracks contain the various bits of sound. The final embarrassment came towards the end of the dubbing process when the mixer stopped and asked me what sound effect was represented by a particular orange line. He then smiled, ran his finger across the page and said "No problem - it's marmalade."

I blushed again at the memory of it when I was asked to read a proof of this book. Would the curse of Mardale return? I'm happy to report that it didn't. Accomplished and rounded as it is, I assume none of the book's contributors have felt it necessary to skip the country. In fact they should stay and take the praise due to them for producing a fine piece of local history. More than that, they've produced a book which is entertaining and readable which, sadly, so many worthy local history volumes that lumber across my desk are not.

Mardale, in this version, is a great tale well told and a credit to the local history society which has worked so hard to bring the details of its story to a wider public. Oh, and not a whiff of stale cheese sandwich nor a smear of marmalade to be found.

Eric Robson

Editor's Preface

Shap Local History Society was founded in March 2001 with the aim of collecting together and recording the vast amount of archive material relating to the parish - documents, maps, wills, photographs, oral and family histories. The Society also has a monthly programme of talks, with outings in the summer months to places of local historical interest, and a fund raising social event at the end of the year.

In 2002 Eden District Council leased the Market Cross building in the Main Street, Shap, formerly the Library, to the Parish Council, who agreed to share the building with the Society as a Heritage Centre. This gave the Society a base for its archives, and a grant from the Lottery Awards for All funding for community groups enabled the purchase of computer and digital recording equipment. An exhibition is held every summer on a local topic: recently these have included Shap in Victorian Times, Shap at Work and Leisure, the Railway through Shap, with the most popular exhibitions being Mardale in 2004 and Mardale Homesteads in 2010.

The Heritage Centre is also open on selected weekends during the winter months for local and family history research. In 2006 a grant from the Heritage Lottery Fund enabled the Society to purchase the freehold of the Market Cross building, and with a further grant from Awards for All, the computer equipment was upgraded and internet access for family history research provided. The grant also included funds to be used towards the publication of a book.

There has been continued interest in the 'Lost village' of Mardale, particularly in drought years when a drop in water levels reveals the stone walls and remains of buildings. In 1995 the drought coincided with an exhibition organised by St Michael's Church. Intended only to run for a weekend, the exhibition attracted visitors throughout the summer and the narrow road alongside Haweswater to Mardale Head was overwhelmed by cars. Over the years several booklets have been published and recently the Society has been given access to the archival material owned by John Graham, whose late wife was the daughter of the last landlord of Mardale's Dun Bull Inn. In this book we draw together previous information on Mardale, include more recent research and family histories, and the material from John Graham's valuable archive.

The Society will be grateful to learn of additional information for the archives, and of course any errors which may have crept into this book.

Liz Amos
Shap, Cumbria
May 2011

View of Measand with Measand Beck Falls in the background

Introduction

"A hamlet unforgettable for the charm of its romantic beauty and seclusion from the world"
A G Bradley[1]

The Mardale valley is situated on the eastern edge of the Lake District, four miles due west of Shap and 15 miles south of Penrith, and contains the most easterly of the Lake District lakes, Haweswater. There are several opinions on the origin of this name. It may be a corruption of Halls Water, referring to Thornthwaite Hall or be derived from Old Norse 'Hafr's Water' – 'Hafr' being a Norse personal name which also means goat. Hawes also means neck – the narrows between High Water and Low Water where the two parts of the lake, prior to the building of the reservoir, were divided by the delta which built up where Measand Beck entered the lake.

Today Haweswater serves as a reservoir for the city of Manchester. The reservoir is four miles long, with a maximum depth of 187 feet, and is also the highest and most isolated lake of the Lake District at 810 feet above sea level. The valley is surrounded by mountains – to the south Harter Fell, and to the west the High Street range – which cuts the valley off from Windermere and Ullswater. The High Street range is traversed by a Roman road of the same name.

Two passes lead southwards – Nan Bield on the western side of Harter Fell rises to 2,296 feet before descending to Kentmere, and Gatescarth, in the shadow of the crags of Harter Fell, which rises to a height of 2,132 feet and down to the valley of Longsleddale on the eastern side. Both these passes were used by travellers on their way to Shap Abbey, and continued to be used by drovers, traders and packmen after the abbey was dissolved, thus avoiding the charges on the Heron-Syke Turnpike route to Shap. The only road, built to replace the one on the western shore which was lost when the valley was flooded, comes from Bampton and follows the eastern edge of the lake past the Haweswater Hotel to a car park at Mardale Head.

High Street from Harter Fell

View of Haweswater from the summit of Harter Fell looking north

A third pass, known as the Corpse Road, leads eastwards over Mardale Common into Swindale and on to Shap. The first steep part of this route can be seen rising in a series of zig-zags up the fellside from the new road. The track was also used for transporting peat to the valley and passes the ruins of three stone huts, which were used for drying and storing peat cut from the upland bogs.

When the reservoir was created during the late 1930s the church and homesteads of the village of Mardale were demolished and the first hollow buttress dam in the world, 1,550 feet long and 96 feet high, was constructed at the northern end of the valley.

Haweswater, and the valley it occupies, owes its shape and form to the underlying rock. Beneath the valley and surrounding fells are the hard and impervious rocks of the Borrowdale Volcanic series, formed some 450 million years ago. These were sculpted by the plucking and grinding of ice during successive glacial periods over the next two million years. As the ice moved downhill the valley was deepened, and some of the side valleys were left 'hanging'. The valley of Measand Beck is an example, and ended in a great spread of boulders and gravel which projected into the lake dividing it into High Water and Low Water. The Measand delta disappeared when the dam was built and the water level rose. The movement of the ice also created corrie basins containing small lakes held by a rock sill, or boulder moraine left by the glacier, such as Blea Water, over 200 feet deep (the deepest tarn in the Lake District), and Small Water. The valley slopes are steep and scree covered and a sharp contrast with the flat plateau tops of mountains such as High Street.

The valley and reservoir are now owned by United Utilities as their Haweswater estate, and the RSPB manage the Naddle Forest Nature Reserve and Site of Special Scientific Interest, with a viewing platform for the golden eagles in Riggindale. Woodpeckers, peregrine falcons and sparrow hawks have been recorded in the woodland areas, ring ouzels, wheatears and warblers in more open areas, and dippers at the lake's edge and becks. In the spring goosanders breed on the lake and during the winter months gulls roost overnight. Red grouse and curlew breed in the higher moorland habitats and there is a colony of small mountain ringlet butterflies. A rare fish, the schelly, is found in the lake. The Arctic char has also been recorded.

The natural lowland vegetation growing on the fertile valley bottoms, river and lake sides has disappeared under the waters of the reservoir, though there are some remnants of this below the dam. The woodlands are rich and luxuriant and probably once covered both sides of the valley. Higher up the vegetation changes to heathland, juniper and acidic grassland with bracken. The big stands of juniper, known locally as the Savins, found on Mardale Common are impressive and can be seen from the road. High up on the fells, beneath High Street, there are areas of rare montagne vegetation, with arctic alpines and tall herbs growing on the mountain ledges.

There are three blocks of semi-natural woodland in the valley, Low Forest and Guerness Wood where oak, birch, rowan, holly and hazel are found with bluebells, wood anemone, dog's mercury and wild strawberry as ground flora. Bilberry is found higher up the slopes of this woodland as the soil becomes more acidic. High Forest and Mirkside contain valley alder and small areas of ash and hazel woodland, ramsons, wood crane's bill, meadowsweet and water avens are found here. On the wet peaty soils near the dam, the third area of woodland consists of alder and willow with areas of sedge and bog moss swamp. Plants found here include marsh valerian, marsh hawk's beard and globeflower. All three areas of woodland contain many species of mosses, lichens and bryophytes. Non-wooded areas of the valley include areas of juniper scrub, upland heath and grasslands.

Before the reservoir was built the landscape was very different. Haweswater was a natural lake, three miles long and half a mile broad, lying in a trough of hills that rose in height towards the lake head under which the village of Mardale nestled. The valley was approached from Bampton by a narrow twisting road which followed the west side of the lake, past the isolated farmhouse of Colby and the settlement of Measand, to Mardale Green.

The road had two good bridges, considered by the Royal Commission to be at least of 17th century origin. Chapel Bridge was near the church and spanned the Mardale Beck. The other was at Measand over the Measand Beck.

Chapel Bridge

In the spring primroses, violets and bluebells could be seen growing by the wayside and, in the summer, wild roses and foxgloves. Willow, gorse, hawthorn and blackthorn, alpine strawberries and raspberries and the rowan tree or mountain ash grew in the hedgerows. The woods of Guerness, Naddle and Low Forest covered the slopes to the east of the lake.

The village was on the route from Kendal towards Penrith through Longsleddale and Gatescarth Pass. Another route came from Kentmere up to Nan Bield Pass and the two routes met at Mardale Green. On the west side of the lake there was evidence of an earlier pack horse route, high up on the slope of the fell. From Chapel Hill it went round to Flakehow, Bowderthwaite and Riggindale. There were two bridges over Riggindale Beck, one opposite Field Head and one at Bowderthwaite. At Flakehow this old route joined with the 'modern road' in the farm yard before the modern road was straightened. This made a new piece of road leading from the parsonage to Speaking Crag (named because of the echo from Flakehow Crags). A further section of the road led up to the parsonage, then went down by High and Low Whelter before passing behind the school house. There was a third section leading from Graven Gate to Burnbanks. Much of this 'old road' was incorporated into the fellside track which Manchester Corporation opened to the public in 1930.

From Graven Gate and High House the road followed the fields to cross Measand Beck by a pack horse bridge. This was made of a single huge flagstone, measuring seven foot by two foot nine inches. The old road linked the farms of Bowderthwaite, Riggindale, High House, Sandhill and Colby, perched high on the fell. By 1928 this route was used very little but both ends offered good cart roads with Arnold Bridge at the Mardale end, probably of 17th century origin according to the Royal Commission(2), and at the Bampton end was Naddle Bridge. There would have been a right of way over Naddle Bridge into Naddle Forest for tenants to collect wood.

Today the valley is a favourite spot for bird watchers and

The old road along the west side of lake

Arnold Bridge

walkers and the car park created at the head of the valley is the starting point for walks over Branstree, Harter Fell, Mardale Ill Bell, High Street and Kidsty Pike. The Coast to Coast walk, from St Bees Head to Robin Hood's Bay, follows the western shore of Haweswater. There are many more visitors during times of drought when the water levels drop and the walls and piles of rubble left after the demolition of the homesteads re-appear.

In spite of all the changes Wainwright was able to say in his Pictorial Guide to the Far Eastern Fells *'Mardale is still a noble valley.'*[3]

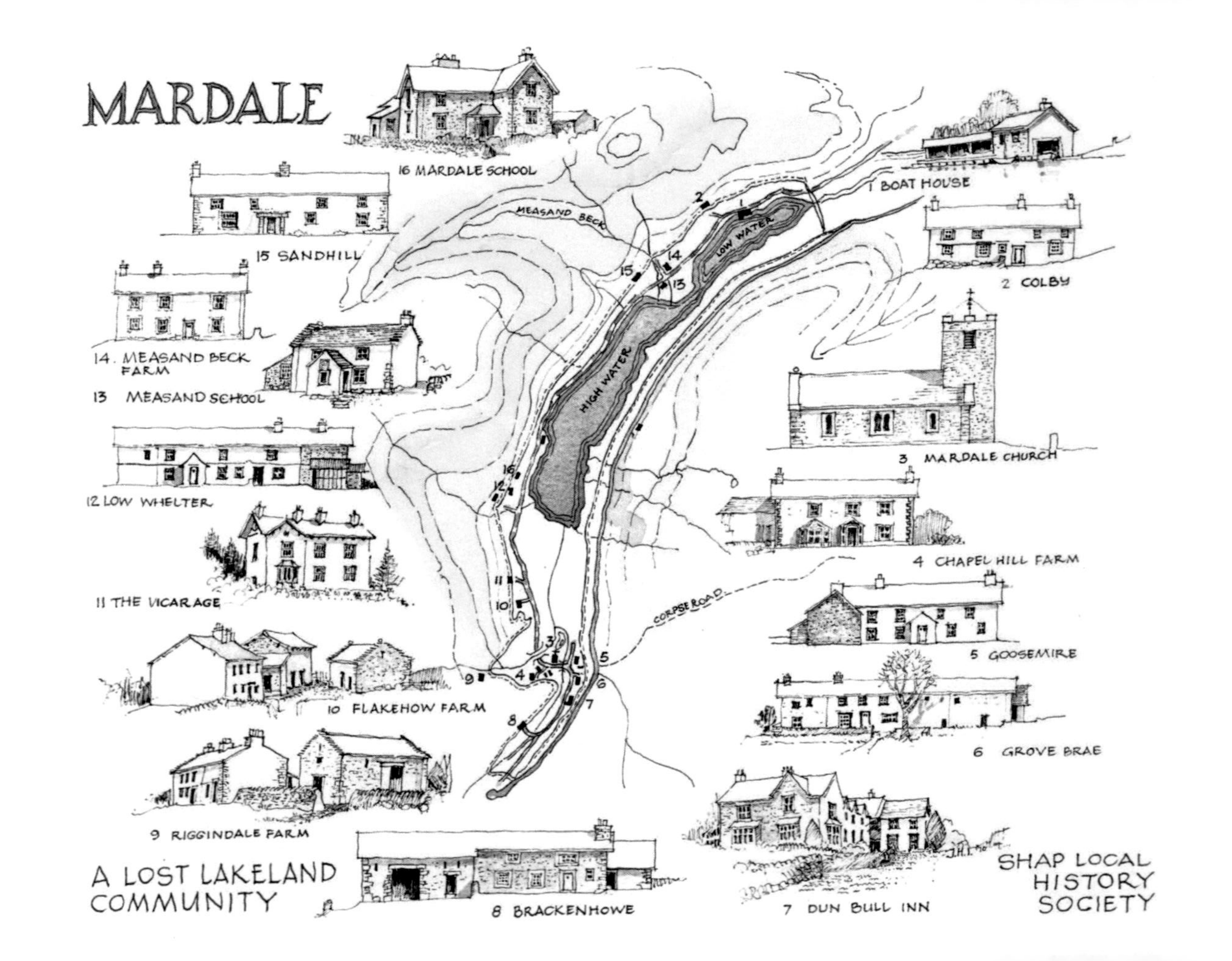
MARDALE
16 MARDALE SCHOOL
1 BOAT HOUSE
2 COLBY
15 SANDHILL
MEASAND BECK
LOW WATER
HIGH WATER
14. MEASAND BECK FARM
13 MEASAND SCHOOL
3 MARDALE CHURCH
12 LOW WHELTER
4 CHAPEL HILL FARM
11 THE VICARAGE
CORPSE ROAD
5 GOOSEMIRE
10 FLAKEHOW FARM
6 GROVE BRAE
9 RIGGINDALE FARM
A LOST LAKELAND COMMUNITY
8 BRACKENHOWE
7 DUN BULL INN
SHAP LOCAL HISTORY SOCIETY

Chapter 1

Early Settlers

Man first arrived in Cumbria some 10,000 years ago, following the animals and plants on which he lived. Originally he set up camps on the coastal plains, using the flints washed up on the shore to make tools. Over thousands of years, as the climate became warmer, explorations were made further inland. By the Neolithic period (4,000–2,500BC), man had arrived along the valleys to what is now known as Penrith and down to Shap and the limestone fells around Orton.

Life here was dangerous - the vegetation was now very dense and it was probably easiest to travel along the less heavily wooded higher ground whilst keeping a wary eye out for any predatory animals. Clearings were made on the uplands by cutting and burning. The remains of burial cairns were found on the fells, and the first clearance cairns, evidence of attempts to use the land for small scale farming.

During the Bronze Age, (2,500–600BC) settlements became more permanent and farming more prevalent. The central fells were still too inhospitable for permanent settlement, but excursions into the higher mountains were made to source suitable materials for making tools. A band of Borrowdale volcanic rock ran centrally through Cumbria, from Scafell to High Street and the Shap fells. This stone was used to make large, heavy tools such as axes, ideal for the heavy and monotonous job of tree-felling to clear more land for settlement. These axes appear to have been brought down from the higher fells in bulk, roughly shaped, to be finished elsewhere.

The area along the Eden Valley contains one of the heaviest concentrations of surviving prehistoric sites in Britain. Stone circles, avenues and cairns, have to various degrees survived the demands of agriculture and are highly visible. The arrival of the Celts around 600 BC brought new farming methods and a new language, a fore-runner of modern Welsh, which included their method of counting sheep and other elements found in local place names.

The Celts also brought the skill of working iron, which was important in providing stronger tools for clearing the land, especially the more densely wooded valley floors. Their Iron Age settlements have left distinctive traces on the ground - stone-built roundhouses within small, walled, farm fields. Cereals were grown on a small scale around the houses, in enclosures to protect the crop from livestock, and the sheep were taken on to the fells for summer pasture. The Celts also farmed a small type of pig, and their cattle were reputedly good milkers called "Celtic Shorthorns". The Celts measured their wealth by the number of cattle they owned, and these were highly prized. These Iron Age settlements lasted well into the Roman period although the Celtic style of house building does not seem to have been influenced by the Romans here in the north.

In Mardale, farming settlement was limited by the steep valley sides to Mardale Green, Riggindale, and the lake shore. Local historian, Mary Noble, tells of a visit to a site above Burnbanks, '*a small platform of rock, very steep on two sides, and with the traces of a wall on the part where it is accessible. It may have been a rock shelter, and certainly it is too small for a sheep shelter.*'[1] Two Iron Age settlements have been found at Burnbanks, with another slightly higher on the fell. Higher still there is an early burial cairn and the remains of field systems and several other cairns of unknown dates. A hut circle and several cairns remain at Little Birkhouse Hill.

Miss Noble also describes a walk to the Four Stones site, where she found '*two standing stones, looking like forgotten gateposts of the roughest description. They are about four feet high, and not set in the ground. Consequently the frequent rubbing of sheep has worn away the ground, and they are now much out of the perpendicular. Two similar stones not far away seem to have fallen from this cause.*'[2] Two standing stones, each at least four and a half feet high, and two large cairns (over 36 feet in diameter) remain today and there are further remains of enclosures and cairns at Mile Crags.

Old Ordnance Survey maps show the remains of a fort at

Measand. A report by the Royal Commission in 1936 describes a site of about one third of an acre, containing two roughly rhomboidal enclosures (see picture). This was later identified as a Romano British farmstead but unfortunately is now submerged in the lake.

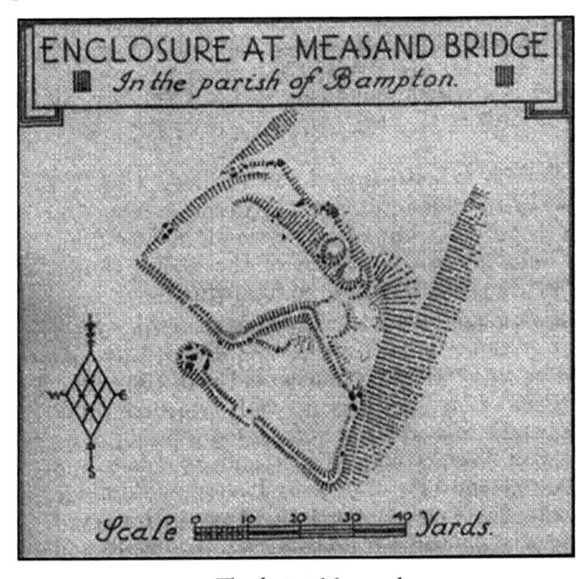

The fort at Measand

Mary Noble also writes of remains at Whelter Coombe. The father and son team of archaeologists, William and Robin Collingwood, excavated these in 1922, identifying the remains of two shielings or shelters, typical of those used to live in by the Vikings when their flocks were grazing up on the fell in summer. The largest hut was 31½ feet x 12½ feet with low platforms at each end which would have been used as bed spaces. The smaller of the two huts originally found was just 13 feet x 11 feet, and was possibly a storage hut. The site was re-examined in 1936 and a third shieling found, another fair sized hut, 21 feet x 13 feet, with walls two and a half feet thick. The three huts are all thought likely to be tenth or eleventh century Norse.

In the same year, 1936, Robin Collingwood excavated the Iron Age hill fort at Castle Crag, some 500 feet above Whelter, on a natural headland. Three of the sides were very steep, and the entrance on the fourth side was up a rocky ledge, so the site itself would have been easy to defend by a small band of men. A ten foot rampart gave additional protection to its summit. There were no traces of buildings or artefacts found, only a level clay floor with traces of trodden-in charcoal and possibly a hearth at one side. It was felt that the lack of buildings meant that the fort was not a permanent settlement but was used only for defence. Did that mean that its occupants lived nearby in the valley and so just used it at times of threat? If someone had gone to the trouble of building a ten foot rampart, it must have been necessary and who were they fighting when it was built? We know that another tribal group lived to the south and west between Windermere and the coast, and that there were other Iron Age settlements over the fell near the head of Kentmere. It is possible that the fort was originally built to guard against raids from the south, over Nan Bield Pass.

Across the lake at Guerness Nab there were several hut circles of another Romano British settlement, but these were probably destroyed by the flooding of the dam and the building of the new road. Another Iron Age or Romano British site, the remains of a small village settlement, was found on the same side of the lake in Low Forest. It was roughly half an acre in size, and had three circular huts surrounded by a field system within a stout enclosure wall of between six and seven feet thick.

The Romans arrived. Apart from their roads and forts, there is little visible evidence of their time here, and no place names. Essentially, Cumbria at this time was a military zone. The ancient track above Mardale was reinforced and 'upgraded' to High Street, connecting the Roman forts at Ambleside and Brougham. The people of Mardale may have been aware of the movements of military troops and supplies along the ridge, but life in the valley may have changed little except that taxes were now paid to the Romans, probably in kind as grain, livestock and hides. The improved roads would have made transport and trade easier, and the market, which had evolved around the Roman fort at Brougham, would have been a source of wonder, displaying a new range of vegetables, herbs, fruit,

Shieling in Whelter Coombe

Castle Crag

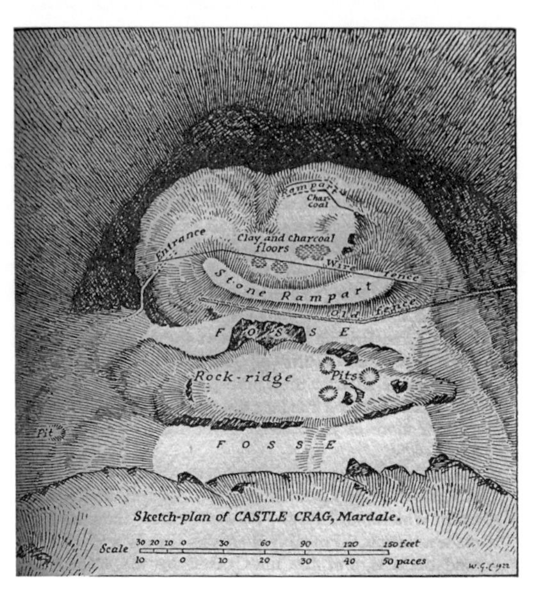

Sketch plan of Castle Crag, Mardale

white cattle, chickens, pheasants – although they may not have reached the table of the average family in Mardale.

After the Romans left, this area was again torn apart for more than a thousand years, by Saxons, Scots, Danes, Vikings, and Normans. Little is as yet known of the earlier years, although soil samples have shown substantial pollen evidence that hops and hemp were being produced in the valley some time around 600AD. From the tenth century onwards, Haweswater began to acquire its Norse place names, not just the general terms such as 'beck' (stream), 'dale' (valley), 'tarn' (small lake), 'ness' (headland), 'thwaite' (clearing) but individual place names as well: Mardale was the 'Lake Valley'; Haweswater, the lake with the narrow strait; 'Harter Fell' was the 'hill of the hart'; and Selside was the 'pasture with a mountain hut'. White Raise, on the High Street path, was actually a tumulus cairn that was reached by Kidsty Pike, the 'steep path', along Riggindale, the 'ridged dale'. Harrop Pike was the 'Craggy Peak', and Guerness where the fishing-traps were set. Gatescarth was named later as the 'road pass.'

Chapter 2

The Manor of Thornthwaite

Mardale was part of Thornthwaite Forest within the Manor of Thornthwaite, a large area encompassing Swindale, Mosedale, Heltondale and the demesne lands at Thornthwaite Hall. The parishes of Shap and Bampton were divided by a boundary which ran down the middle of Haweswater. It was a remote, agricultural community with most of the land consisting of upland pasture. The Lords of the Manor were mainly absentee landlords with major holdings in other Cumbrian manors more prosperous than Thornthwaite. The lands of Mardale were 'sublet' to their tenants in return for services and rent.

The Curwens (formerly de Culwen) of Workington Hall held the Manor of Thornthwaite from the 13th century for over 300 years. Although the violence and devastation of Scots raids was a persistent worry, no pele tower was built in the valley during this time. Mardale and Haweswater were possibly more sheltered from these raids, being hidden away from the rest of the manor lands which lay nearer the open plain of the Eden Valley.

Mardale was, however, on a major packhorse route connecting the Eden Valley with Kendal. South of the Gatescarth Pass in Longsleddale a pele tower was built circa 1450 at Yewbarrow Hall, and south of the Nan Bield Pass. There was a fourteenth century pele tower at Kentmere Hall, at the head of the Kentmere valley. The families owning these halls presumably felt the need to protect themselves from northern raids. A pele tower, with walls three and a half feet thick, was eventually built in the northeast of the Haweswater valley at Thornthwaite Hall in about 1576 because one of the Curwen family was about to make a home there.

From the records of the Manor Court it would appear that life in the valley was an oasis of tranquillity. The Court was held twice a year and dealt with changes of tenancy, local disputes and minor offences, and a Court Baron was held every three weeks or so, when tenants could recover small debts within the manor by paying an entrance fee of 4d – 1d to appear and 1d for a verdict. Tenants held their properties by Customary Tenantright, which gave much of the security of a freehold: property descended to the eldest son or heir for the same rent and terms, and they even had the right to sell their leases as long as changes were recorded at the Manor Court. The tenants of Haweswater were allowed necessary timber for repairs and materials for thatching and they also had rights on the Common, both of Pasture and Turbary, and *'Stone and Slate on the waste ways'*[1] for repairs. Turbary was the right to cut peat. In 1772, Henry Rooke Esq, brother and heir of John Rooke, deceased, applied to take over his messuage and tenement in Mardale, *'according to the custom of the manor'*.[2] The rent was 5s 3d and 'greenhew' 2d. Greenhew was a common payment for the right to cut green wood and brushwood for fuel.

Since Norman times at least, tenants owed the manor a number of services, or 'boons', apart from the rent. Boons were days to be worked on the Lord of the Manor's demesne, the lands he reserved for his own farm, and were recorded at the Manor Court as the number of days mowing or ploughing owed by each tenant. In later times, when the Manor Lord's farm was leased to a tenant farmer, the boon days were no longer needed and so were exchanged for a cash payment. It appears that manor tenants also had a duty to provide a number of hens to the Manor Lord each year. A seventeenth century document shows that the Lord of Thornthwaite Manor received from his tenants a total of 82 hens per year at Christmas! This seems to have been a widespread custom: Burn and Nicholson record *'pout-hens'*[3] for other parishes through Westmorland along with the number of days mowing or ploughing owed by each tenant. At a later date, this duty seems to have been commuted to a monetary payment of 6d for each hen owed. A list, dated 1774,[4] of boons for the manor shows 49 days mowing valued at 1s per day, and 7¼ days ploughing valued at 4s a day. A similar list dated 1810 shows boon hens still at 6d each and a day's mowing unchanged, but a day's

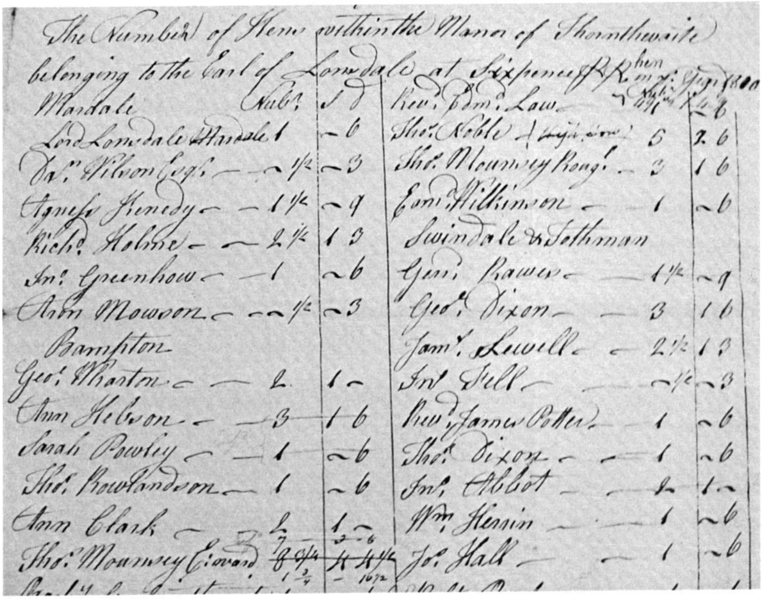
The Number of Hens within the Manor of Thornthwaite belonging to the Earl of Lonsdale at Sixpence each ... 1810

Mardale		s d			
Lord Lonsdale Mardale	1	– 6	Rev. Edm. Law		
Dan. Wilson Esq.	½	– 3	Thos. Noble	5	2 6
Agnes Kennedy	1½	– 9	Thos. Mounsey	3	1 6
Richd. Holme	2½	1 3	Edm. Wilkinson	1	– 6
Jno. Greenhow	1	– 6	Swindale		
Ann Mowson	½	– 3	Geo.	1½	– 9
Bampton			Geo. Dixon	3	1 6
Geo. Wharton	2	1 –	Jam.	2½	1 3
Ann Hebson	3	1 6	Jno. Bell	½	– 3
Sarah Powley	1	– 6	Rev. James Potter	1	– 6
Thos. Rowlandson	1	– 6	Thos. Dixon	1	– 6
Ann Clark	2	1 –	Jno. Abbot	2	1 –
Thos. Mounsey Edward			Wm.	1	– 6
			Jos. Hall	1	– 6

Boon hens in the Manor of Thornthwaite 1810

ploughing was now reduced to 2s. The list reveals another oddity, that a tenant (here, Daniel Wilson) could be due to pay just half of a hen!

Cornage was an Anglo Saxon term, recorded either as a kind of tax on horned cattle or the duty to blow a horn to warn of raiding Scots. In Mardale it may be more likely to refer to the latter. After the Union of Crowns in 1603, the need for the service fell out of use, and by the eighteenth century it had been replaced by a money payment. A list of Mardale tenants, dated 1741, shows the major landholders of each area, paying Nowtgeld or Neatgeld, another name for cornage: Matthew Wright for 'Couby', Water End and Seal Green, Mary Holme for Flakehow, John Holme for Riggindale, John Cookson, Richard Jackson and John Holme for Mardale, and one unnamed person for Bowderthwaite.

The annual rents appeared to be low. In 1559, Roger Salkeld of 'Meson' was recorded as taking over his father's tenement in Measand, the rent being 8s per year, the equivalent of £94.70p in 2008. But circumstances could change. In June 1808, there is a record of one of a block of properties being taken on by the one man:

'Thornthwaite/Bampton Patrick: The Court Baron and Customary Court of Dimissions of the Right Honourable William, Earl of Lonsdale, Lord of the said Manor, held at Bampton Grange, for the said manor, on Friday the seventeenth day of June 1808 before John Richardson, Esquire, Steward of the said Manor.

To this court came Thomas Mounsey of East Ward, only Son and Heir at Law of Christopher Mounsey deceased and prayed to take of the Lord of the said Manor A Messuage and Tenement situate at Meason with the appurtenances within the said manor, of the yearly Customary Rent of three shillings and three pence, formerly Curwen's.'[5]

The remainder of the above document contains many terms stressing the fact that the land is not freehold, *'prayed to take of the Lord', 'Customary Rent', 'according to the Custom of the Manor', 'always reserving unto .... '*. The yearly rent is 3s 3d and the Admittance Fine, a one-off payment due when taking on a property, was ten times the amount of the rent. The document reminds the tenant of other services due and of a complication – a General Fine always had to be paid on the death of a Lord of the Manor, which equated to a sum of ten times the annual rent. The Admittance Fine was a predictable fee, paid when taking on a tenancy. The General Fine was less predictable as to when it would be due, and could be the final blow for tenants with less available money. In this particular case, the manor had been purchased from another family by Lord Lowther, as opposed to being inherited following a death. The previous Lord from whom he had bought the manor was still alive, so when that former Lord died, there would be a General Fine to pay. If the tenants were unlucky enough to also lose their new Lord of the Manor in the near future, there would then be two General Fines to pay within a short time, the equivalent of twenty years rent.

Less than two months later, on 28th July 1808, the documents show that a General Fine was levied due to the death of the previous Lord. Thomas Mounsey, paying for several Bampton properties as well as the two properties taken on at Measand, was now landed with a General Fine of £25 15s 10d. John Wharton of Mardale, who normally paid just 2s a year for a messuage and tenement, now had to pay £1 for his fine. John Greenhow, paying for Greenhead, Garthbeck and Brackenhowe, paid a General Fine of £9 2s 6d. Richard Holme, the heir of the Holme family, was now apparently managing the family affairs, his father John being in his eighties. He was paying for a messuage and tenement at Mardale (rent 16s 6d), a messuage and tenement at Bowtherthwaite (14s 6d) various parcels of land, and two messuages and tenements at Chapel Hill (12s 10½d and 7s). Holme was now faced with a General Fine of £29 13s 4d.

Women were able to rent land in their own right. Agnes, wife of Thomas Kennedy, was paying £1 0s 1d for a messuage and tenement in Riggindale in 1808 and was now levied £10 0s 10d for her General Fine. Sarah, wife of Joseph Powley and only child and heiress of the Reverend Richard Hebson, had taken a garth 'wherein Meason School now stands' with appurtenances for 2d per year, whilst Ann Hebson, presumably another relative, had several messuages, tenements and parcels of ground at nearby Colby Seel Green.(6)

The manorial records are important to family historians as they contain pre-census information not easily available elsewhere. Jane Hayton, daughter and heir of George (deceased) took over Goosemire in 1818 for a rent of £1 1s per year with a £10 10s Admittance fine. Ann Wharton, only daughter and heiress of George Wharton, deceased, took on his messuage and tenement at 'Measonbeck' in 1825 for 10s rent, £5 fine. Frances Kennedy of London, spinster, eldest daughter and customary heir to the late Agnes, wife of Thomas Kennedy, deceased, took on her 'messuage and tenement situate in Riggindale'(£1 0s 1d) in 1835. In 1839 Maria Antoinette, spinster, eldest sister and customary heir of Frances Kennedy, late of London, deceased, asked to take her messuage and tenement in Riggindale, rent £1 0s 1s. John Holme of Mardale, yeoman, eldest son and customary heir of Richard, late of the same place, yeoman, deceased, takes a messuage and tenement at Mardale (16s 6d), at Bowderthwaite (14s 6d), and two at Chapel Hill, (7s, and 12s 10½d) – there is a possibility that he was paying for all branches of the family.

There had always been fishing in the valley – the name 'Guerness' means 'fishing trap headland'. All the fish in the manor belonged to the Manor Lord, even the wild fish in the beck, and fishing rights were let by licence. The two small tarns above Mardale, Small Water and Blea Water, as well as Haweswater itself, were recorded as being well stocked with trout and mid eighteenth century the fishery in Low Water, Haweswater, was recorded as let for 5s per annum.[(7)]

There was other industry apart from farming. Records show that there had been a water driven corn mill at Naddle. Timber and mineral rights were also reserved to the Lord of the Manor. Although Lord William Howard had searched for coal in 1618 without luck, the 1782 sales catalogue for the manor describes valuable veins of lead and copper ore, and there were several copper mine workings around Mardale and small amounts of iron ore.

Various outcrops of slate were productive. The slate was a fine blue variety and high quality. Two quarries, one in Mosedale and the other at Mardale Waters, were let to the Rawes family and worked for some years. In 1776 Sir Edward Hassell granted Robert Rawes a seven year lease of the slate quarries at Mosedale, including the *'farmhold'* at Mosedale, grazing at Mardale Waters *'except for 10 cattlegates there belonging to Daniel Wilson'*, and *'any slate quarried therein.'*[(8)] The Mardale Waters quarry was clearly productive for slate as it was specifically named in the 1783 lease renewal. Between Mosedale and Mardale Waters quarrying was a substantial business. In 1815 William Rawes, son of Robert of Mardale, yeoman, was apprenticed to Messrs Hodgson, Atkinson & Hodgson, Slaters, of Carlisle and County Durham, *'to learn the trade and business of riving, tearing, and Dressing of blue slaytes in their Slate Quarries at Mardale Waters or elsewhere.'*[(9)] The slate was used for roofing many houses around the county and further afield.

Receipts charged to the Manor of Thornthwaite in the mid eighteenth century and retained in the Lowther Archive, give a fascinating insight on the prices of the day, and it is interesting to speculate where the work was being done. For one job, the following was required:[10]

for wharling stone, 4 pens a yeard [sic]	
5 skore and 16 yeards which cometh to	£1 18s 8d
For leding stone and wood	£3 0s 0d
for fetching freestone	£0 11s 0d
for fetching boards	£0 5s 0d
for 20 lod of lime	£1 3s 4d
fetching 24 cart load of sand	£0 10s 0d
for drink Bread and Buter	£0 1s 6d
a stone of harc	£0 1s 2d
to dressing Ground work	£0 12s 0d
	in all £7 17s 0d

(NB This total is as copied from the document, but actually adds up to £8 2s 8d)

Another bill, dated 4th June 1746, is for work done by Edward Ion, Richard Relph and John Tinklar:

walling, 116 yards	£2 3s 6d
to chimney pipe	6s 0d
to slating and pointing slate & walls	£1 19s 6d
	in all £4 8s 0d

There is also a receipt signed "received by me John Langhan" and dated 15 September 1746, for 32½ foot of glass at 7d per foot at a cost of 18s 11½d.

This was a lot of glass. Sir Edward Hassell, Lord of the Manor at this time, was keen on building new farmhouses as well as restoring Dalemain, his mansion near Ullswater, and it is possible that the repairs or new building here were due to his influence. It is not known if the glass mentioned above was part of the same job – the sheer amount used implies that it was for a substantial new house.

There are a number of receipts specifically naming Naddle, all recording payment of the bills by one Leneard Whitesmith, possibly the estate steward or tenant at Naddle, for *'the yous [use] of Edward Hassell.'*(11)

William Rawes, 20th September £3 1s 4d for slate and leading for Naddle

Joseph Robinson, 22nd September 5s for 'three dubble carts and four single ones'

Thomas Wilson and his men for work at Naddle, forty-three days, £2 4s 0d, and his painters for six days work £0 3s 0d.

John Bowman 'for flagging a house at Nadell', 30 yards at 4d a yard – 10s, and three days work – 3s

John Tinkler [sic] for Iron work for the 'new house at Naddle', 22 September 1746, as follows:

2 strong door crooks	£0 1s 4d
a door sneck	£0 0s 6d
2 strong clasps holdin door checks with	£0 1s 2d
spiking	0s 6d
more spiking	0s 6d
3 stone 1½ pounds of new iron for stanchers	7s 9d
Drawling and Curling to window stanchers this iron	2s 6d
Door handle latchet & stapel	1s 4d
2 strong door bands	2s 4d
nails for	0s 2d
3 door bands from Mill Howe & 3 crooks and nails for them	1s 3d

Wood was valuable, and it was not permitted to fell trees without a licence, or to take the wood away. In 1722 it was recorded that some tenants had been arrested – William Noble for cutting and felling and Roger Harrison and Matthew Thompson for *'buying and carrying from the customary lands of William Noble without leave or Licence of Francis Warwick, Lord of the Manor of Thornthwaite.'*(12) This point of law was reinforced in 1797, when the Right Honourable James, Earl of Lonsdale and then Lord 'of the said Manor' issued a warning via the Manor Court, that there was no right to cut down, sell or dispose of any timber or wood growing on customary estates, tenants being allowed only such as shall be allowed to them by the Lord or Bailiff for repairs to their customary tenements.

Other penalties were imposed for stray animals – the owners of any tethered or loose cattle found in Whelter Field would be fined 6d for every default. Unauthorised enclosures were another potential problem. Farmers sometimes found it convenient to 'move' walls to gain a little more land. In 1674 the court found that William Aray *'hath taken a part of the afore said forest and that the jury doth sett downe that he shall take his wall in againe and set it where it were before and lay the ground upen before Lady day next upon paine of 3s 4d.'*(13)

Despite being, in the main, absentee landlords, the various landed families who owned the Manor of Thornthwaite did make their own mark on the valley. In 1576, Sir Henry Curwen, then Lord of the Manor, had upset a dozen of his customary tenants by ousting them in favour of his son, Nicholas, who was about to be married. He had wanted to provide the young couple with their own home at Thornthwaite. From the document it appears he had considered the demesne land at Thornthwaite Hall to be insufficient to their status, and had enclosed the twelve tenants' lands with it, adding the pele tower to 'cap' the whole. Thornthwaite Hall was later described as *'an Elizabethan mansion on rather a substantial scale.'*(14) The tenants took him to court, complaining bitterly of the fact that they had held the land 'according to ancient custom' in consideration of their readiness to do border service at their own cost. As it was feared that the tenants could refuse to fulfil their border duties, the case was referred to the Privy Council in 1576, although it would appear that Sir Henry got his own way.

The Dissolution of Shap Abbey, the only Abbey in Westmorland and one of the last to survive, had taken place in 1540. The English monarch was now head of the Anglican church, so to oppose the Anglican church was to oppose the monarch. Catholics became increasingly subject to persecution, constantly under suspicion of treason and plotting against the Crown. The Manor of Thornthwaite, from Norman times until the eighteenth century, had been held by three main families, the Curwens, the Howards and the Warwicks. The Curwen family had held the Manor from the thirteenth century. The last

(Curwen) Lord of the Manor, Sir Nicholas (whose father had built the Hall for him at Thornthwaite), had had Catholic sympathies in his youth which he appeared later to recant, possibly for political expediency. Sir Nicholas sold the Manor around 1610 to Sir William Howard, who was also to live at Thornthwaite Hall for several years while his new home, Naworth Castle, was being rebuilt. This new Lord of the Manor, known as 'Belted Will', was constantly in trouble with the government for his Catholic faith and for being on the wrong (Royalist) side during the Civil War. His tenants, including those of the Manor of Thornthwaite, were fined huge amounts by Parliament as a result, again resorting to the courts in an attempt to ameliorate the situation. In 1679, a later William Howard and his wife, of the parish of Bampton, may have used the February weather as an excuse when it was recorded that they were unable to travel to take the Oath of Allegiance. The manor passed eventually by marriage to the Warwick family of Warwick Bridge, also Catholics.

Records were also kept by at parish level of those not attending the Anglican church, and heavy fines (and often prison sentences) were imposed on all Non-Conformist manor residents, whether Catholic or Protestant. The financial pressure to conform forced most to comply, but even in the latter half of the seventeenth century there remained a stubborn core of Mardale individuals, Aireys, Barwicks and Haytons, who held out against attending the Anglican service.

In the eighteenth century the manor was held by Sir Francis Warwick of Warwick Bridge, who sold most of the land in 1772 to Edward Hasell of Dalemain, keeping just Thornthwaite Hall for his own use. By 1777 Sir Edward was in dispute with the tenants of Thornthwaite Manor: the tenants resorted to legal advice, complaining that he and Sir Francis Warwick (the latter still resident at the Hall) were cutting down the wood on the demesne lands and on the waste, so depriving them of wood for their repairs. They also complained that he was neglecting to hold the Manor Courts, so that they were forced to pay for special courts to decide matters. However, before the case could come to court, Sir Edward died, and Thornthwaite Manor was

The Thornthwaite tenants bid at Penrith Sale, 1782

put up for sale by auction. The manor tenants combined to bid in an attempt to buy their freedom, and made an offer of £2,958. This was refused but the Hassell family said that if they could raise £3,200, they would accept the offer. The tenants were unable to do so and the opportunity was lost.

Edward Hassell Esq, Sir Edward's second son, acquired the manor, but it was rapidly sold again, to Sir James Lowther, Earl of Lonsdale, known as 'Wicked Jimmy', and in Lowther hands it was to stay.

Chapter 3

Traditional Life, Customs and Legends

Traditional Life

Sketch of a Mardale kitchen by A. Reginald Smith, RWS

Life in Mardale changed little over the centuries – it was a self sufficient community where the folk lived by their own means, just as their forbears had done. In high summer the dale head was in the sunshine from mid morning, when the sun rose over the shoulder of Harter Fell, until late afternoon, when it slipped behind Kidsty Pike. In mid winter the valley head did not see the sun for several weeks as it tracked its course low in the southern sky.

The sturdy farmsteads had huge inglenook fireplaces, with a large lath and plaster larder where sides of mutton, beef, bacon or ham could be hung for preservation in the smoke from the fire. The fire was the heart of the home, and was carefully managed so it did not go out, for it provided warmth and the heat to cook food. It was not unknown for folk to brag that they had their grandfather's fire. The fire was heaped with slightly damp turfs at the end of the day, to keep it smouldering until next morning when the addition of some dry 'elding' or kindling soon created a blaze.

In Mardale the main fuels were peat and wood, and the remains of peat houses at the top of Hopgill can be seen close to the Corpse Road. The peat was cut during the summer months, dried by the sun and wind, and was stored in these buildings ready for winter when loads were brought down the steep hillside on wooden sleds. There was also a plentiful supply of firewood with the ancient forests of Naddle and Guerness close at hand.

The family sat within the inglenook during the evening, exchanging news and telling stirring tales of people and events long ago, at the same time doing other tasks, the menfolk making or repairing 'hare nets', mending their footwear or carding wool whilst the womenfolk were spinning, knitting stockings, sewing or making rag rugs. These capacious chimneys were very draughty, so the men often wore their hats to protect themselves from 'hallan drops' - sooty rain or hailstones which came down the chimney. The wearing of hats indoors continued long after these great open fire places were filled in and the fire replaced with a Victorian range.

The light was provided by resh leets, these were peeled rushes dipped in tallow, or mutton fat, the result being similar to a thin taper, which had to be burned at a forty-five degree angle. The resh leet stands that have survived are of iron on a wooden base, and have pincers for holding the resh leet. Occasionally extra light was required for some close work so the candle would be bent in half and both ends lit - hence the saying 'burning the candle at both ends'. Sometimes a glass bowl of water was placed in front of the flame to increase the illumination. At a later date, thicker tallow or beeswax candles became available and later still, paraffin lamps.

The traditional clothing was homespun, woven from the wool of the farm's own sheep - the fleece of the native Herdwick with its natural grey colour - to produce the hardwearing 'hodden grey' cloth. The weatherproof garments made from this cloth were virtually indestructible - there are many instances of hodden grey coats and jackets being handed down from father to son.

Furniture was made from oak and was very basic. Most homes had a large table, with benches or three legged 'coppy' stools, and occasionally a stout armchair. There was also a 'kist' for storing meal. Beds were frames with a tight rope mesh to support a horse hair mattress and if they were lucky, a feather

Spinning gallery at Naddle

or chaff bed. The covering would have been woollen happins.

There was little change to this hard working life style until the early nineteenth century when new developments reached them. Most inhabitants did not travel further than Bampton or Shap, with the longest journey undertaken being to the market in Penrith.

A Mardale man lamented the poor physique of latter day dales men by saying that *'There is neah folk nowadays to what they war; what, fooak used te be a yerd atween t'shooders and a foot atween t'een"*[1] There were still strapping sons of Mardale at the beginning of the twentieth century - Willie and Isaac Greenhow, Tom Edmondson and Joe Mounsey. These men, ruddy with health, bore stout testimony to the value of a shepherd's life.

The running of a farm was normally done by the family, but on larger establishments, or those where there were few sons, men and girls were hired at a local hiring fair. Womenfolk normally looked after tasks such as cooking, and cleaning, milking and dairying, peat cutting, spinning, weaving, knitting, making clothes, rush lights and soap. The menfolk saw to the running of the farm, outdoor work and heavy tasks such as chopping wood.

The valley people relied upon what they could produce – meat from sheep and the few pigs, some beef, whilst poultry provided both eggs and meat. Bread was made from oats in the form of haver bread, sometimes called clapbread. (There is a slight variance in the way this is cooked, clapbread is slapped onto a hot stone or griddle and allowed to dry whereas haver bread was flattened and baked in an oven.) Oats, and barley, which was grown in smaller quantities, were the only grain crops able to survive the climate. A limited supply of vegetables, such as peas, beans, kale and some root crops were grown in the garden ground close to the house. The introduction of turnips as a root crop in the mid eighteenth century meant that the tradition of slaughtering of cattle before winter was no longer necessary, as cattle could be fed with turnips and maintained throughout the winter. Barley was also used for brewing. Occasionally the family meal would be a 'treat' in the form of fish from one of the numerous becks, or a red deer which had strayed over from Martindale and not returned.

Whilst there were vast acres of rough grazing for sheep, there was also some dairy farming, although the amount of grazing land on the valley floor was limited. In about 1865 Harriet Martineau is said to have recorded that each week 30 hundredweight of butter was collected from the farms of Mardale by carrier's wagon and taken to Shap station for transportation to Manchester.

There are several other references claiming 3,000 pounds of butter being sent from Mardale to the big cities every week, but they do not indicate the source of the information. However the Visitors Book at the Dun Bull for the year 1858 has an entry for Luke Biggins from Sheffield. The same man visited the following year and described himself as '*Luke Biggins, No 11 Flatt Street, Sheffield. Butter, milk deale'r*, and then at the end adds '*Tallow Works*.'

Although the amounts of butter mentioned seem incredible for such a small community to produce on a weekly basis, the fact that a butter dealer was visiting Mardale indicates that the valley was considered sufficiently productive. It is likely that he would travel all over the farming community, perhaps into Bampton too, seeking supplies, and the amounts quoted may be what left Shap Station each week, not necessarily all of it from Mardale.

Horses were used widely, and yeoman farmers made primitive horse collars or 'braffins' of hay and straw, and bridles from hemp cord, or plaited seeves (rushes) were used. A 'sonk' or green sod fastened in place with hay or straw bands was used as a saddle. Leather saddles and harness were deemed to be 'showy' and only used by the more affluent landowners. Sleds were used for transporting goods in the steep fields and fellsides. Early wheeled transport consisted of crudely fashioned wooden carts known as 'tummel (tumbrel) cars' with two solid wooden wheels fixed to the axles - these cumbersome vehicles were in use until the end of the eighteenth century.

Hay was an important part of the winter fodder rations, and a few farms also grew hemp for making into ropes. Threshing was done on a 'burying cloth' (a dried horse skin) which was thrown onto the barn floor and the grain threshed by hand, using a flail. In the spring the ploughing began and, after the last frosts, oats were sown and potatoes planted in trenches.

Lambing time was a busy period. The lambs had to be protected from the worst of the weather, so the fell flocks always lambed late in the spring having been brought down into the 'intak' for easier supervision.

If yance they git milk and can wander about,
They care not for frost nor for snow;
For it's plenty o' suckle 'at gars them git stout,
To skip, and to lowp, and to grow.

By the end of May the pastures were grazed bare by the ewes and lambs, which were then sent back to the fell. These bare pastures had little grazing left so were shut up to allow the grass to grow again. Peat was cut in June, which gave it a long time to dry, and it was turned from time to time, a job allocated to the children.

In July the sheep were washed, and then clipped. All the local farmers gave a boon hand to get the job done. Gwendolen Garston recounted an incident on clipping day at Flakehow:

'A young man from Bampton passing the farmyard leant over the wall and for a joke shouted some rude words at "ye dirty suavers!" In a flash all the men were up, seized their sticks and beat him, chasing him right off the farm boundaries. It is an old tradition that it will bring ill luck to the flock to curse the sauving process, going back to a very old tradition that healing is a sacred process.'[2]

Clipping days were always noisy, lively gatherings.

Sek bleatin' o'lambs and sek barkin' o dogs,
Sek jybin and jwoking o' men;
Sek clatterin' o lads in their old caulkered clogs,
Sek drinkin' o' whisky. Amen!

The day was followed by a supper with singing, dancing and some sport such as wrestling. Most local lads were skilled in Cumberland and Westmorland style wrestling and despite a late finish, many would manage to rise early next day for another day's clipping to be followed by a similar evening.

To help a good neighbour at his merry meeting,
A whole country side to employ;
In housing and clipping with much friendly greeting,
For clippings are meetings of joy.

Haymaking took place in August. The workers rose early,

Clipping day at Goosemire

took a rest at mid-day and worked late into the evening, often by moonlight.

Now mowers can't work through the middle of the day,
For the biting of clegs and for heat,
So they snoozle some hours in the new cut hay,
And make up by working at neet.

During the following days the hay was allowed to wilt, turned, shaken out, formed into rows then gathered into hay cocks of ever increasing size before being made into pikes ready to transport to the hay mew in the barn or field house. On some farms rectangular stacks were built in the stack yard, these were well thatched to keep out the weather.

Harvest time was in September and after the main part of the crop had been gathered, the last of it was left standing for the custom of 'shearing out'. The corn (the local name for oats or havver) left standing was enough to hold with one hand and the heads were tied together, the reapers threw their sickles at it from a designated point, the 'luck' going to the one who managed to cut it down. As this last sheaf was bound in the field, someone would shout the traditional exclamation 'That's

John Edmondson and his father haymaking at Flakehow

t' yan we've bin leuking fer aw harvest!' This final sheaf was known as the 'luck sheaf' and was safely stored with an apple in it until Christmas morning when the apple was given to the youngest daughter and the sheaf to the best dairy cow – practices with links to pagan rituals.

The end of harvest was celebrated with a Kern Supper, the word 'kern' is believed to be a derivation of 'corn'. This gathering, for all the workers, friends and neighbours, took place in a barn with a supper followed by a dance, the master of the farm first dancing with the girl who carried the 'luck sheaf' from the harvest field and the mistress with the head man or servant.

There was a lull in the work during October, November and December and this was when events such as the Shepherds Meets, Merry Neets, Taffy Joins and Auld Wives Hakes were held. A Merry Neet was a social gathering which usually involved feasting, drinking, dancing, singing and card playing. A Taffy Join was a social gathering when toffee was made in a pan, and was often used for match making when mothers tried to get their daughters linked up with eligible bachelors. An Auld Wives Hake was an annual gathering, usually around Christmas, which was attended by both sexes – the women drank tea, ate cake and gossiped whilst the men played cards or attended a cock fight in the locality.

Sheep salving took place in October. The sheep's fleece was smeared with Stockholm tar or salve which was a mixture of rancid butter, or any other available grease, mixed with tar (pine resin) and rubbed well into the skin. This was absorbed throughout the fleece, and was the method in common use for repelling pests before the introduction of dipping, which did not come into practice until the end of the nineteenth century. This job was often done by itinerant workers known as 'scab doctors'; it was slow work but a good man could do twenty sheep in a day. Some farms had salving houses where the operation was carried out – low buildings with an open side to allow air to circulate. After the introduction of compulsory dipping in 1906 many of these were demolished or adapted for other uses.

A fleece smeared with salve was known as 'tarry woo'. It was difficult to work with due to the amount of salve in the wool. Although spinners say they need some grease (or lanolin) in the wool for it to spin better, it would be virtually impossible to spin wool that was caked with Stockholm tar without first washing and carding it. This wool would often be discarded as unfit for spinning, but with some time and patience it could be worked upon and spun to produce something of value, and a bonus for those willing to put in the effort since wool was a valuable commodity.

This song was traditionally sung at the Mardale Shepherds Meet and was the first song following the Loyal Toast.

Tarry Woo'! O Tarry Woo'! Tarry Woo' is ill to spin;
Card it weel! O card it weel! Card it weel ere you begin;
When it's carded roll'd and spun, then your work is but half done;
But when woven, dress'd and clean, it may be clothing for a queen.

Martinmas in November was one of the traditional times for hiring fairs, the other time being at Whitsun. The big events, held in Penrith and Kendal, attracted sideshows and fairground rides. It is recorded that smaller gatherings were held at Annas Cross (Annette Cross)[3] along the lake shore near Whelter.

Youths and men stood about with a straw in their mouth as a sign that they were for hire. In some places lads would stand on one side of the street and lasses on the other. Farmers would wander among them and ask 'Are you for hire me lad?' They were hired for a six month period for a payment of four or five pounds, the bargain being sealed with a luck penny or 'arles'. Once this was accepted, the hired person was required to turn up at the new place of employment on the agreed day, and failure to do so would mean that the employer could demand the agreed year or half year wage back from the hired lad or lass's parents. Some farms were good hiring spots, others were bad ones, and the reputations of each farm were passed around among the servants. When the half year was up the master would sometimes ask the farm servants to stop on, and make a new bargain with them.

In December oats were prepared for milling, and preparations were made for Christmas. The winter months were often long and hard, with farmers having to carry fodder to the hill sheep and digging them out of snowdrifts.

Wood was a valuable commodity, with the larger trunks and branches used for construction, whilst thinner branches were used to produce charcoal. In January 1749 Mr Edward Hassell of Dalemain set up an agreement with Isaac Walker, Edmund Ion, John Robinson and Richard Walker who would be known as colliers, *'for the felling and cutting into proper lengths a certain quantity of underwood at Thornthwaite; all oak, ash, elm and holly'*(4)

The agreement then states that *'all wood six inches over and upwards is to be riven into pieces for coaling and be about four feet long, and the wood that is under six inches to be cut into three foot lengths all the wood to be laid about the pitsteads where they were to be 'coaled'*; that is, made into charcoal. Mr Hasell agreed to pay 3s 10d for every dozen bags of charcoal produced, the bags to be filled five foot in height and well shaken down.

There are many traces of pitsteads in Guerness and Naddle forests. Charcoal burning took place in the summer months; the wood was peeled, and the bark used for tanning. The sizes of wood coaled were known as 'shanklings' and 'coalwood'. A circular pit about fifteen to thirty feet in diameter was prepared on level ground with a large single pole or 'motty peg' set upright at its centre; the cut timber was stacked around it to form a beehive shaped pile, about six feet high, and this was covered with bracken and a layer of turf. To start the burn the central peg was removed and a shovelful of glowing charcoal tipped in, the burn starting at the centre of the stack. The hole at the top was sealed with a sod; too much air would burn the wood away and produce wood ash instead of charcoal. The colliers built crude conical huts covered with sods to live in. The burn would take between one and three days, and several burns could be in progress at the same time. When the coaling was done the stack was 'sayed' with water to produce steam and cool it, and the charcoal was raked out to cool before being shovelled into sacks. Each pitstead would produce about two and a half dozen sacks.

There was also a copper mine in Guerness with a cluster of buildings, the smelted ore would have been traded somewhere locally such as Kendal. The bloomery for smelting used the charcoal available close at hand.

The dalesfolk conversed in the local dialect. Dialect is a vernacular speech form that differs from standard English in both syntax and idiom: it is not slang and many words have Celtic and Scandinavian origins. In Mardale a variation of the local Westmorland dialect was spoken, which had its own peculiarities. No natural speakers of the Mardale dialect now survive, but the last of them was recorded for posterity in sound and on film.

Scandinavians from Norway and Iceland settled in the valleys of Cumbria during the ninth and tenth centuries. They were second and third generation settlers who came via the Isle of Man and their words can be found in many local place names and distinctive words in the local dialect. There are also some Celtic survivals, such as the sheep scoring numerals. Dialect words are also used to describe the landscape – *how* for a hill, *crag* for a rocky outcrop, and *dub* for a pool are Celtic words, as are *girn* – a fish trap and *gurr* – muddy, which with *ness* for headland are found in Guerness. Names such as *brant* for steep (as in Branstree); *fell* for mountain, *dale* for valley, *beck* for a stream, *force* for a waterfall, *mere* for lake and *tarn* for a mountain lake, and *thwaite* for a clearing are all derived from the Scandinavian languages.

Tommy Edmondson, born and raised at Flakehow, was a great raconteur and native dialect speaker. After the flooding, he moved to Shap, where he lived until the 1970s, when he moved to Penrith. At the age of 92, he was recorded on tape telling tales about the Mardale of his youth. He told four tales and here are two of them:[5]

'Ther' was this chap as ' ta' Mardle Shepherd Meet, he c' fra oot ' Ken'mer – Nowble Walker, he co' ivvery year 'n' h'd git a gey lot o' beer, 'n' stoppt' t' weekend. Ennyrwoad, he gat '' click wid a John Hebson as warked fer t' Manchister Cwooperashun. Th''d suppt beer aw t' day, n' then when t' neet com, suppt whisky aw neet. Furst yan

went t' bar, 'n' than t' uther, 'n' when aboot sebben er eight o' clock o' t' mwornin' John Hebson went fer them agen, he fetched hissel a pint dash back. Nowble says "Wat's ta ganna dea wid that – ista ganna hev a wesh?" He says "Nay, Ah's ganna sup't." "Weel", Nowble says "If thoo sups that efter aw that whisky, i'll blaw th' brains oot!" Anan he says "Nay,'t' ll nut – cos thoo nivver hed enny.'

~~~~~~~~~

'Lordy used ta com up, he wasn't a fisherman, but he liked ta sail roond t' lower lake ta view t' scenery, 'n' h'd allus com twa er three times i' t' summer, 'n' sail aroond. Ennyrwoad the'd landed back tull t' bwoathoose, an' his bwoatman was a bit durty – he used te brag as he'd nivver hed a wesh fer a month. Lordy likely saw as he was durty, sea when the' gat back ta t' bwoathoose, Lordy says "What a beautiful stag that is, right on the skyline, up Walla Crag." T' bwoatman says "I don't see it mi' Lord."

"Yes" Lordy says. "He's yonder, good enough to be seen, a fine stag; he must have six or eight points." "Ah don't see it mi Lord." "Well", Lordy says, "He's good enough to see, just beyond that holly bush." "Nay, Ah still can't see 't m' Lord." "Well then stand up in the boat, and then you can't help but see him." Sea t' bwoatman stood up i' t' bwoat, Lordy gev't a rock, t' bwoatman popped in. Lordy says "That's right get a good wash you dirty devil!" '

The Celtic sheep scoring numerals are well recorded, and similar systems can be found in Wales, Cornwall and Brittany. The numbers only go from one to twenty – a score. Flocks were referred to as so-many score.

1	**Yan**	11	Yan-a-dick
2	Tyan	12	Tyan-a-dick
3	Tethera	13	Tethera-dick
4	Methera	14	Methera-dick
5	**Pimp**	15	**Bumfit**
6	Sethera	16	Yan-a-bumfit
7	Lethera	17	Tyan-a-bumfit
8	Hovera	18	Tethera-bumfit
9	Dovera	19	Methera-bumfit
10	**Dick**	20	**Gigot**
~~~~~~~~~

Some of the following dialect words are still used in connection with sheep:

Yow or Yowe – Ewe**; Tip, Tup or Teaap –** Ram; **Gimmer** – a young female sheep; **Hogg –** a young sheep between five and 14 months old; **Twinter** – nearly two years old (having seen two winters).

There was also a system of marking the sheep from each farm with 'smit' marks, usually coloured, which ranged from letters to 'pops'. There were also ear marks known as 'lug marks' – notches and slits cut into the ears of the sheep – branding on the face and finally horn burns; these were recorded in Shepherd Guides to aid identification. These marks would be of great value at the Mardale Shepherds Meet.(6)

Chapel Hill (Holme): Upper halved both ears, H on far side, H burned on face.

Dun Bull (left) Under halved far, cross on near side.

Grove Brae Pop on shoulder, stroke over fillets and down both lisks, A on face.

Goosemire Cropped near, under halved far, stroke down far shoulder, like mark down tail head.

Brackenhowe Forked near, stroke down near shoulder, stroke from fillets to tail head.

Flakehow (Edmondson) Cropped near, under fold bitted far, stroke down buttock. Twinters: red behind head, face burned on far cheek.

Whelter (i) Cropped near, stroke down near shoulder, G on face. (ii) Cropped and slit near, under fold bitted far, stroke down shoulder.

Measand Beck (Kitching) Under halved near, cropped far, pop in fillets, K on far side, K burned on face.

Thornthwaite Hall (Dargue) i) Black faced; stroke down far shoulder, pop on near hook, T on near horn, the year of our lord on far horn. (ii) Naddle sheep; cropped both ears, burned across face. Herdwick, D on face. (iii) Inland sheep; D on near side, all pop on near hook, stroke down far shoulder.

Mardale, despite being at the head of a Lakeland valley surrounded by impressive high fells, was far from being isolated. The two mountain passes, Nan Bield from Kentmere and Gatescarth from Long Sleddale were main highways between Kendal and Penrith for sheep drovers, packhorse trains, peddlers and all manner of travellers.

In the early years of the 19th century Mardale became part of the theatrical circuit travelled by the famous Charlotte Deans, formerly of Wigton. Mrs Deans was a remarkable woman, twice married and raised seventeen children. She toured the northern counties for over forty years. Mrs Deans and her company made a truly theatrical entrance into Mardale over Nan Bield Pass from Kentmere following performances in Kendal at the turn of the 19th century. There were a number of ponies, some carrying people and others the trappings of the theatre. Her troupe brought colour and excitement to the valley.[7]

In many dales of the Lake District there were statesmen farmers, families who had held land for many centuries from the great estates, and enjoyed what were almost freehold tenancies. In Mardale the only family to qualify for this title were the Holmes family. The statesmen were chiefly sheep farmers, with a heafed flock attached to the farm, and any increase in the flock numbers was by their own endeavours at breeding. They could sell these sheep out of the valley as long as the same size of basic flock was passed to the next tenant or owner.

Mardale people, like all dalesfolk, were hospitable by nature. If anyone called at their home, whether a neighbour or stranger, they would be invited to take some tea or supper with the family, the traditional invitation being 'Noo mek thisen a good tea; reach tull, divvent be flayt, mak a lang arm.'

Note to reader; dialect is written phonetically, so pronounce the words as they appear.

The above reads 'Now make yourself have a good tea, reach to, don't be afraid, make a long arm (ie reach out).'

A Jerry or ale house was also situated at Guerness, run by an old woman who brewed her own beer. The first brew from mash is the most potent with each subsequent brewing being weaker by turn. A tale is related of how a party of young men out hunting came upon the building and enquired about a drink. The old woman offered them Ram Tam, Middle Mow or Pinkie. The men opted for Middle Mow as it seemed to sound moderate in strength. This was stronger than they had anticipated and they staggered out to make their way home with the old woman commenting *'Lor' bless us, if they'd gitten as mich Ram Tam, what wad hev cumt o' them!'*

Customs

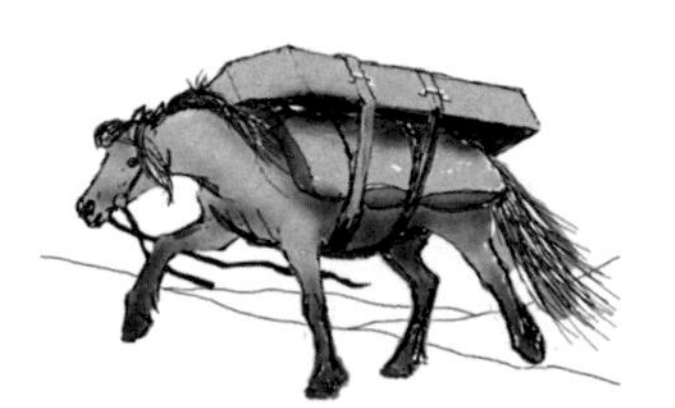

Sketch by Sue Millard

The custom of carrying the dead for burial at Shap by way of the Kirk gate gave rise to legends and stories. Custom has it that Hall Caine in his novel *The Shadow of a Crime* told of an incident on the Mardale Corpse Road. A wicked man had died in Mardale without being shriven. As his coffin, strapped to the back of a horse, was being taken to Shap for burial, a thunderstorm broke and the horse bolted. For three months it roamed on Swindale Common with the coffin still on its back. Eventually it was captured and the man was buried at Shap. Similar tales to this are told about other parts of the Lake District where there are corpse roads, so it cannot with any certainty be claimed solely as a Mardale legend.

However, one that can tells of how the old matriarch of one of the farms died and was taken by the menfolk in the traditional way to Shap for burial. The horse was young and skittish and broke away from the funeral party, turning back towards Mardale. A small child at the farm who had watched the departure of the cortege, saw the returning horse with its burden and shouted *'Mudder, Mudder, Ganny's cu' back.'*

Childbirth was fraught with danger for both mother and child and this continued to be the case during the 19th century with child mortality still being fairly common. Therefore many rituals, charms and superstitions were connected with this episode of life. If a mother rocked an empty cradle there would soon be another baby to fill it, birthmarks were believed to have been caused by a pre-natal contact with a mouse, bat or hare. A popular pastime was to divine the sex of a baby by suspending a wedding ring on a hair over the bump, likewise it was believed that boys were carried high and girls low. Late arrivals were believed to be boys since they took more time to make.

The confinement was women's work, and local women who were experienced in delivering babies were called upon to assist at the birth. The father-to-be invited his male friends to partake in a 'merry meal.' For this meal the mother-to-be would have baked a groaning cake, a rich fruit cake which was cut into the number of slices as there were people present, these were known as 'whangs of luck.'

The mother's bed should not be turned for a month after the birth, and her first day downstairs had to be a Sunday. Before being taken downstairs, the baby had to be taken upstairs, to ensure that it got on in life, so in some cases the midwife would stand on a chair and lift the baby above her head. All hair and nail clippings for the first year had to be burned in case a witch got hold of them and used them in a charm. It was also considered to be unlucky if a child saw its own reflection in a mirror before it was two years old, and this superstition continued within living memory.

It was considered unlucky for a mother to enter another person's house until she had been 'churched', at a service of thanksgiving for childbirth. It was thought that when a baby was taken into a house apart from its own, it would 'smittle' (infect) the woman of the house and she would then become pregnant, therefore the first house visited would often be that of an elderly relative.

Baptism also had its own customs. The best known of these is the serving of rum butter or sweet butter – a mixture of butter for richness, brown sugar for a sweet disposition and rum for the Holy Spirit. It is still traditionally served at christening teas. After the rum butter has been eaten the bowl should be emptied and used to make a collection for the child. A custom that is almost unheard of today is that of a christening piece – this consisted of bread for the necessities of life, cheese for richness of life and a piece of silver for wealth – which was presented to the first person of the opposite sex the baby met on the way to the baptism. During the ceremony, a door (often known as the devil's door) or a window on the north side of the church was left open so that the devil could be cast out, the north side of the church which saw no sunlight being considered the domain of restless souls and evil spirits.

Children played a wide variety of games, many involving chasing, and Mardale children had a wonderful playground for games such as Fox and Hounds. One child, 'the fox', was given a set time in which to run off, they were then hunted by the rest of the group, 'the hounds', with many shouts of 'tally-ho!'

As the children grew into young adults in search of a partner for life there were customs, mainly used by girls, to divine who their intended partner would be. In one well known one, a girl would peel an apple in one long length, then toss it over her shoulder where it would form an initial on the ground. Another involved taking an apple pip between the thumb and first finger and squeezing it whilst reciting *'Pippin, pippin, paradise, show me where my love lies, east, west, north, south Kirkby, Kendal, Cockermouth.'* The pip then flew off in one of the directions. The baking of a 'dumb bannock' was also well known, for this a girl would prepare the dough without speaking, then place it on the griddle before going silently to bed, in her dreams she would see her future husband turning the bannock.

Love tokens also featured; in Cumberland and Westmorland these took the form of a knitting stick, a device that was tucked into the waistband to secure a needle when knitting stockings with four needles, thus leaving one hand free for other tasks.

Sketch of knitting stick, left, by Jean Scott Smith

When the banns were called it was known locally as being *'thrown ower t' pulpit'* or *'hingin in t' bell reapes'*. Weddings were often bidden, when a bidder was sent to *lait up* (find) any who cared to attend the wedding and reception. Guests often raced from the church to the reception on foot or horseback for prizes, which could range from a saddle or spurs to a pair of gloves, depending upon the wealth of the hosts.

The Shepherds Meet, when stray sheep were rounded up for identification, became one of the main gatherings in the valley. Originally the venue was the summit of High Street, where sports and horse racing took place - some old maps name the summit Racecourse Hill, and an old steel etching depicts horse racing with Blea Water below.

It is difficult to imagine the men struggling up the steep fell side with barrels of beer and food, along with their horses -

Steel engraving of horse racing on High Street

how those poor beasts had the wind to race after such an ascent is incredible. The Shepherds Meet eventually became established at the Dun Bull.

There were also the customs common to the neighbourhood, for instance the Easter time custom of Pace Egging, when youths would dress up and go around the local homes performing the Pace Egging play in front of the fire. The play symbolises Christianity and Paganism and light and darkness. The costumes were simple, such as jackets worn inside out, and faces blacked with soot. The weapons were home-made – just sticks cut from the hedgerow. At the end of the play there was an appeal for eggs and money.

The tradition of giving and receiving of Pace Eggs at Easter is widespread, their name comes from 'paschal' meaning Easter. The eggs were hard-boiled and dyed with whatever natural materials were available, such as onion skins, gorse blooms and various wild flowers. The egg is a symbol of new life, the custom being to roll the eggs down a local hill on Easter Monday, the winner being the person with the last intact egg. Mardale church held a special egg tithe.

The tradition of lighting bonfires at various seasons was a Pagan custom that survived until the second half of the 19th century. The Spring festival of Beltane was celebrated on May Day, and there was also a tradition of Midsummer, Halloween and Midwinter Bonfires. Midsummer fires were to celebrate the Summer solstice. After the Gunpowder Plot of 1605, the Halloween and Samhain fires were discontinued in favour of Guy Fawkes night, but the customs of carrying lighted 'tamlets' (lengths of rope soaked in tar) and blazing barrels continued to be observed. The midwinter bonfires were lit at the Winter solstice or Yule, and became part of the Christmas festivities. Celebratory bonfires were still held in Mardale, one in 1897 to mark Queen Victoria's Jubilee, and in 1902, to celebrate the coronation of Edward VII.

Another type of fire that would come into Mardale at various times was the Need Fire. This was kindled, observing strict rules, at times of pestilence as a primitive form of fumigation. All household fires had to be extinguished before a new fire was kindled by friction of wood on wood. It was lit to the eastward, and then passed from farm to farm without fee or reward and always from east to west in the direction of the sun. An account exists of the last time Need Fire was brought over the top into Troutbeck in 1851, and it is likely that this fire would have originated in Mardale. Lots of old thatch, weeds, bracken and so forth were piled onto it to make a smoky fire, then all the livestock from the farm were driven through the smoke and sometimes ailing humans too! Once the operation was complete the embers were used to rekindle the household fires.

Christmas was a great time for celebration, with families visiting one another, sharing food and drink, giving and receiving small gifts, and there would no doubt be some dancing where there was a suitable instrument to provide music. There would often be a group of mummers performing a similar play to the Pace Egging play described earlier.

Legends and Tales

The legends of Mardale are well documented and appear in several books on the subject of the valley, passed on in oral tradition, possibly a survival from the Scandinavian settlers who came in the ninth century and built homesteads in Measand, Whelter and Mardale, with summer saeters on the high ground. Whilst some dismiss tales in the oral tradition as unreliable, we only need to look at the Icelandic Sagas that were not committed to paper until several hundred years after the events they describe, yet researchers have discovered that the information was incredibly precise, so they had lost nothing in the telling and retelling. Therefore do not dismiss the legends of Mardale, however fantastic they may seem – there could be more than a grain of truth in them.

The most famous Mardale legend is that of Hugh de Holme, and his story is told in Chapter 9.

During the time of Border warfare, which continued until 1610, news reached Kendal of an advancing raid, through Mardale and over Nan Bield to Kentmere. The Kendal Archers, who were famous for the part they played in the Battle of

Agincourt, were dispatched to Mardale where they took up positions on and around Castle Crag. The advancing Scots were met by volleys of arrows, and few were left alive. The dead were buried where they fell. Centuries later a few of the disillusioned followers of Bonnie Prince Charlie, in retreat from Derby during severe winter weather, took the route north from Kendal, over Gatescarth or Nan Bield through Mardale, and unwittingly passed the last resting place of their fellow Scotsmen. Whether they escaped the skirmish at Clifton, the gallows at Carlisle, and the horrors of Culloden to make it home to their beloved Highlands and Islands will never be known.

A tale also exists from 1745 when Mardallians saw a cavalcade, complete with carriages and outriders, crossing High Street. When the ground was examined the next day, no sign of hoof or wheel prints were found. The strange coincidence was that, at the time of this spectacle, Prince Charles Edward Stuart was reviewing his troops in the north of the county following his capture of Carlisle. This tale has distinct parallels with the well known legend of the Spectral Army of Souther Fell. (In 1735 a large army was seen moving on the east side of Souther Fell, which is the eastern extremity of Blencathra, to the south of Mungrisdale village. It was seen again in 1737 and again on Midsummer Eve 1745 when 26 people witnessed the army. A search of the area showed no signs of any army having passed that way, some of the terrain being unsuitable to ride over).

The cairn on the top of Hugh Laithes Pike was the burial place of Wicked Jimmy Lowther, whose ghost had terrified the inhabitants of Lowther after his burial there. The vicar had attempted to exorcise his ghost without success, so his remains were exhumed and reburied at the highest point of Naddle Forest. It is said that he rides his horse at breakneck speed down the fellside into the lake.

A tale is also told of how a salesman came into Mardale and tried to sell a Bible to a farmer's wife. She obstinately refused, and at last he gave up remarking that she was a weak woman. *'What,'* she said, *'me a weak woman, wid thirteen barns an' sniggin' wood oot o Guerness twice a week. Me a weak woman!'*

Glossary of the some of the less familiar dialect words used:

resh = rush
happins = blankets
t' een = the eyes
havver = oats
seeves = rushes
gars = makes
sek = such
cleg = horsefly
anan = and then
brag = boast
sea = so
com = came
gaily = very
ista = are you
i' click = paired up with
yan = one
thisen = yourself
sniggin' = dragging
ganna = going to
wesh = wash
lait = search/find
scale = to scatter, spread
divvent = don't
mek/mak = make
kist = chest
fooak = folk
yerd = yard
braffin = horse collar
intak = walled enclosure
lowp = leap
jybin = teasing
fra = from
bwoatman = boatman
allus = always
co' = come
deun = done
gey = considerable
Ken'mer = Kentmere
furst = first
sebben = seven
flait = afraid
hissel = himself
dea = do
nivver = never
reapes = ropes
tull = to
flayt = afraid/frightened
lang = long

Chapter 4

Mardale Homesteads

Evidence of early occupation in the Mardale area can be seen in the many tumuli, cairns and standing stones on the surrounding fells. There are traces of what were thought to be the ruins of Romano-British farmsteads at Naddle, on the delta at Measand and at Guerness. The earliest dwellings in the Mardale valley would have been very primitive.

The Norse settlers influenced the architecture as they infiltrated the valley. Between their arrival and late medieval times the dwellings became more sophisticated with a cruck frame, which rested on a stone base, to support the roof. The walls were probably stone rather than wattle and daub. The roof was thatched with heather (ling) - slate as a roofing material was not widely used until the seventeenth century. Animals were housed in rough stone shelters with roofs thatched in a similar way to the houses.

Very few substantial dwellings existed in the valley before 1600. The years from 1650 to 1700 were the time of 'the big rebuild' in the Lake District as the Union of the Crowns, the cessation of the Border raids and a more favourable climate gave rise to a more prosperous and settled period. Customary Tenants were also more secure after changes in the laws of tenancy.

All but two of the last inhabited dwellings in Mardale date back to this rebuild time. These dwellings may have been built on the footprint of the early buildings but it is more likely that they were built alongside the old places, which seemed to have continued in use for many years after, gradually falling into total ruin and disappearing, in most cases altogether.

The older cruck beam arrangement of the early dwellings was replaced by roof trusses supported by the walls of the houses which now had two storeys. The beams and old timbers from the early houses were valuable and were often reused in the new buildings. Slate, mined close by in Mosedale, was used to roof all the 17th century houses. Most of them had crow-steps on either end to give extra strength to the roofs in stormy times. These disappeared gradually over the ensuing years when the roofs were renewed or re-slated with only a few remaining in place at the time the farmsteads were demolished.

Most of the seventeenth century houses followed the same style of the cross passage arrangement. One end of the cross passage gave access to the firehouse, the main room, which was partly shielded by a partition or heck along which stood a wooden bench or long settle. The houses all had large inglenook fireplaces which stretched across most of the wall. A fire hood made from lath and plaster extended up into the chimney in which meat was hung for smoking. This hood could be accessed from the room above as well as from the fireplace. There was usually a cupboard, often with a carved and dated door, in the fireplace wall, known as a spice cupboard. Another cupboard was sometimes built into the fabric of the house which separated the firehouse off from a little parlour. These cupboards had up to six doors on three levels and were called a brideswain, or more recently, a court cupboard. Many of them were carved with the initials of the owners.

The dwellings in Mardale were grouped into settlements which developed in areas of the valley where there was enough land to create the big shared field which was the typical method of land use up until the eighteenth century.

The following descriptions of the homesteads are preceded by a description in italics taken from the RCHME Survey of 1935.(1)

Naddle (Naddale) The name is derived from the word *'neet'* meaning cattle.

'The house is first mentioned in the Church Registers in 1590 and appears to be very much of that date. The original house is the rectangular block S of and including the main chimney stack. Early in the 17thC an addition was made at the N end; to be followed later in the same century by a wing and a stair in the angle between it and the original house. In the early half of the 18thC the byre and stabling were added at the S end of the early building. The interior has stop chamfered

ceiling beams and exposed joists. The fireplace to the original building is deeply recessed, and has a big flue of plastered timber framing which is carried up, pyramidal fashion, to a square flue of stone at first floor level supported on wooden corbelling. The NE addition has a wooden partition wall with moulded vertical boarding. The chimney breasts in this room have shaped and moulded corbelling supporting the mantel. The staircase has shaped 'splat' balusters. The roof has tie beams with diagonal struts and two sided purlins.'

Remnants of an ancient village are evident among the woodland at the foot of Naddle, evidence of the very early occupation of the dale.

Naddle

Only Naddle House survived into the early twentieth century. It is situated on the north eastern flank of the valley, in a small dale of its own. The house bears a date near the doorway TW 1792 which refers to Thomas Wilson who extended the house. It is possible that Naddle Farm was originally a Hall House and was the principal dwelling in the settlement.

According to records in the church registers in the late 16th century, several families were living in Naddle. The Jacksons are recorded there until at least 1609 and the Wilsons may have been there for many more years, the last entry being in 1760 when detailed records ceased. At the same time there were also families by the name of Chappelhow, Craston, Atkinson and Dennison living there. Thomas Stewardson, a member of one of the oldest families in Shap Parish, also lived at Naddle where he made his will on 5th March 1712.

There were remains of dwellings near the foot of the lake as well as opposite Measand on the old track which ran along the eastern shore, all within Naddle, providing homes for all the families recorded there. Naddal occurs as a personal name in the Shap registers from 1582 when the baptisms of Elizabeth, John and Mabel, children of Robert Naddal, then living in Rosgill, are recorded. No doubt these were the descendants of the old family who took their name from Naddle in the days before parish registers began. An isolated entry in 1704 records the death of John Naddle son of William. The name no longer exists locally.

By the early part of the 19th century whatever smallholdings and dwellings had existed in the settlement were absorbed into Naddle Farm. In 1851 the family of Joseph Green were in occupation. Joseph was from a family which came into Measand from Martindale around 1750. Jossie Green and his son left Naddle to farm near Orton. After the Green family left, George Greenhow, a shepherd, and his family took up occupation and were still living there in 1901. Naddle House was well out of the way of the destruction created by the flooding of Mardale and, still occupied, it sits peacefully in its own dale.

MEASAND

(Meason) This name is derived from mere (lake) and sand describing the large sandy bank or peninsula which reached out from Measand Falls and almost cut the lake into two at a place called the Straits.

From the earliest registers there is evidence of a substantial population in Measand. Names cannot be ascribed to places in these early documents but Colby, Sandhill, Laythalt, High House, Seal Green, Mellbecks and Measand Hall are all included in the settlement which is said to have been the favoured place of the Norse settlers. In 1660 the following Customary Tenants were recorded:

1 Meason; 3 Wrights; 3 Hodgsons; 1 Noble; and 1 Aray.

Some of the early smallholdings were no more than seven or eight acres and gradually became unviable. One by one they were all abandoned and became one large entity, Measand Beck Farm. Meason(d) as a personal name appears in the Shap registers from 1563 and in the Bampton registers from 1641, the last record being that of the wedding of John Measand of Rased and Jaine Jackson of Mardale on the 10th July 1690.

Seal Green This name means Willow Tree Meadow. The smallholding was down a lane from Colby by the edge of the lake and the land was absorbed into Colby at an early date. It was the home of the Wright family before they moved to Colby. The only record of it in the church registers as a dwelling was when Mary Wright died there in March 1729. In a field on the north east of Measand known as Killands there were some earthworks known as 'the Fort'.

Colby *'The house is first mentioned in the Church registers in 1694 and was probably built very shortly before that date. The windows have chamfered joints but the mullions which show in the heads of the larger openings have been cut away. The S. gable is crow stepped. The interior has chamfered ceiling beams and exposed joists. North east of the house is a 17thC barn built of rubble and with stone slates. The ends of the barn have crow stepped gables. The roof is in three bays, with crutch trusses springing from half the height of the walls; two side purlins and ties halved into the principals.'*

According to the Bampton registers William, son of William Hoggert, was born here when it was known as Cowby Fold. A barn or cottage behind Colby farmhouse had a date stone inscribed 17 MSW 33 which referred to Matthew and Sarah Wright who came to Colby sometime before 1726 and probably rebuilt the ancient dwelling. At this time it was known as Colby Folds or Colby in Measand. Matthew Wright was allocated pew 58 in Bampton Church in 1726.

The practice of keeping place names in the registers ceased

Colby

Sandhill

at this time in the Bampton registers and it is not until the 1841 census that we can say for certain that Henry Nevison and his family were in residence. It is interesting to note that Jonathan Rigg, aged 40, the school master at Measand School was lodging with them. Jonathan was born at Crosby Ravensworth, the Riggs being an old established family there. He later married and lived at Sandhills. The Steadman family were farming there in 1861 and were followed by Robert Kitching and his family who were at Colby until at least 1901.

On some old maps Colby is marked as 'Abbey' which may be an error but could be evidence of some connection with Shap Abbey. One possibility is that it may have been an outlying hospital or tithe barn. On the fells above the house there are some standing stones and the remains of copper mines. The last occupants of Colby before it was demolished were the daughters of Tom Edmondson of Flakehow. The ruins of Colby still remain above the high watermark of the reservoir.

Sandhill This name is descriptive of its location, being on the lower fellside above the Measand peninsular.

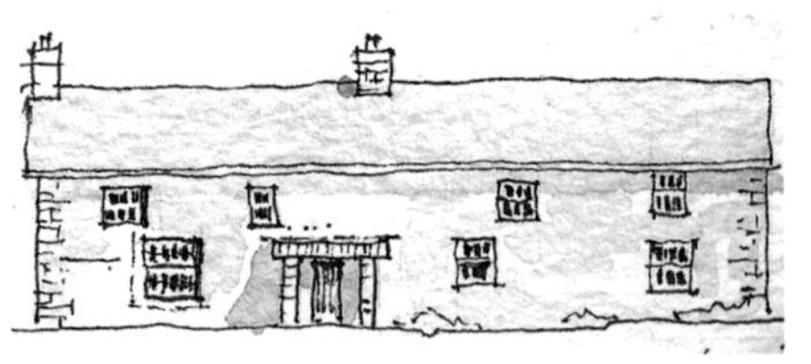

'Built in the late 17thC/ early 18thC. There is a blocked fire window at the SW end of the SE wall. The staircase is contained in a rounded projection in the NW wall. All windows have modern frames. There are no old internal features.'

The first recorded family at Sandhill is that of Thomas Holme in 1712 and it may be that he built Sandhill. The family had a long association with the property, the last record being that of the baptism of John Holme, son of John Holme, in 1758. Richard Wright died there in November 1716, the church register recording that *"he founded ye school at Measand"*. He had lived at Sandhills in the care of the Holme family.

The Green family came to Sandhill in the mid 1700s and in 1841 John Jackson was farming there with his family. One of his granddaughters, Sarah, later Mrs Newton, lived to be 100 years old. In 1851 Thomas Kitching was living at Sandhill, having moved his family to Mardale from Kentmere. He eventually went to live at Measand Beck.

From 1861 until the late 1870s Sandhill was home of Jonathan Rigg, probably the last master of Measand School. From 1881 it was the home of William Kitching, 'the Boatman' and his large family of elegantly named children.

Jane and Isabella Kitching at Sandhill

Measand Beck Hall This property was built in 1839 by the Reverend Thomas Stanley Bowstead around the same time as the 'new

Measand Beck Hall

house' at Chapel Hill. These were the only two houses in the valley built in the 19th century. Thomas Stanley Bowstead was the nephew of John Bowstead, the 'Master of Measand', who is mentioned in Chapter 7. The only other family to occupy the house were the Blands.

Laythalt (Laythald, Laithwaite, and Lathead*)* This name is derived from the old Norse for bridge on a track.

Laythalt was a substantial holding which lay on the west side of the road, south of Measand. Many of the higher field walls can be seen well above the present high water mark. In common with most of the homesteads in Mardale there were often two or more families recorded as living in one place. This is explained by the fact that some of the many small cottages which existed with their holdings from earlier times continued in use well after the 17th century surge of rebuilding. These small holdings may have had only seven to ten acres and were taken in by the larger unit once they had become unviable. This was the fate of the farm at Laythalt as it was eventually absorbed by Low Whelter and Measand Beck Farm. The dwellings gradually disappeared and by 1928 only a barn remained.

The first recorded occupation of Laythalt shows Henry Lowis and his family living there. Henry was of the old Shap family who may have arrived at Shap around the same time that Hugh Holme came into Mardale. In 1726 Henry Jnr was allocated a seat in pew 65 in Bampton Church. The descendants of Henry Lowis were recorded for the last time at Laythalt in 1762 when Hannah, the wife of Thomas, died aged 84. Thomas, son of Henry and Anne Holme, was born at Laythalt in 1731 and this family were followed by John and Margaret Hoggart who were recorded here for at least 40 years. The Ions and Wharton families also had holdings here.

Measand Beck Farm – also called Mellbecks in Measand ie *'amidst or amell ye rivulets'*. The farm lay on the east side of the road at the head of the Measand peninsular.

The house was not recorded in the RCHME 1935 survey as the surveyors judged it to have been built before 1700 and it was not possible to date its origins exactly. However, in 1714 George Wharton married Mary Blamire of Mellbecks and they proceeded to raise a family there until George died in 1741. George was allocated a seat in pew 65 at Bampton church in 1726.

There are no firm records of the occupiers between 1741 and the 1841 census, when John and Margaret Douthwaite farmed there. In 1851 Richard and Margaret Mounsey were the tenants. In 1852 Thomas Kitching and his family arrived at Measand Beck Farm and farmed there until he died in 1892. He was succeeded by his son, Thomas, who continued the family occupation until the flooding of the valley.

High House in MEASAND *'The northern end, originally the dwelling house is now in ruins. The southern end comprising the barn and two storied byre is of the second half the17thC. It is gabled at the N. and S. ends and has a roof in five bays, with stop chamfered tie beams and two side purlins. The floor at the S. end of the building is carried on stop chamfered beams.'*

The house dated to the seventeenth century but was in ruins by the early twentieth century and absorbed early on into Measand Beck Farm. The barn was used as an outhouse. In 1726 James Greenup of High House was allocated a seat in pew 65 in Bampton church. John and Mary Ion are recorded here in 1734 and Agnes, wife to John Brown, died here in 1857.

WHELTER

This name is derived from the Old Norse *'Whelt'* for a hollow or a coombe and *'er'* meaning sheiling. The settlement lies below Whelter Coombe, a huge dish shaped hollow in the western range of mountains reaching from the shores of Haweswater at Whelter Knotts to Whelter Craggs 1,200 feet above. Farms in this settlement included High and Low Whelter, Rowan Park and Slapestones.

Rowan Park or Mountain Ash Park.

'The house, comprising the southern half of the building is of early half of the 17th C; the barn and byres at the N. end, being added a little

Rowan Park

later in the same century. The roofs to this northern part have been almost entirely rebuilt in recent years. The S gable is crow stepped. The first floor to the southernmost part of the house has been removed with the exception of the stop chamfered beams. The fireplace has a circular, stone lined oven. This room and the adjoining room to the N have the remains of a large timber framed hood or flue to the hearth, fitting into stone flues at the top of the wall. The stone flues are carried on corbels. The roof to this part of the building is of tie beam and side purlin construction. On the N Side is a staircase, rounded externally also.'

Standing by the roadside north of Whelter, this ancient dwelling was built between 1601 and 1625. It still had the outside turret staircase, and the enormous chimney and inglenook with the lath and plaster smoking larder, when it was demolished. This fireplace was five foot wide by ten foot long by six foot high. Rowan Park is only mentioned once by name in the registers when John, son of James and Agnes Halton, (Hayton) of Rowland Park, was baptised in 1752.

One of the Baily family recounted a story about Rowan Park in the Baily family newspaper:

'At the time when the big fell walls were being built, the wall at the top of High Street, along the head of Riggindale, was built by two brothers named Sharpe. They lived at Rowan Park, which must have been 'going down' as a farm house then. They lived in one room, and

their horse did not get too much to eat. One day it was hungry and got into their room and ate their chaff bed! While they were building the wall at the head of Riggindale they had the horse and cart up there to load stones. One day they loosed the horse out and there came a great gust of wind, which blew the cart right over the edge and down into Sale Pot where it arrived in bits. Rowan Park had a stone or brick oven, the kind that you put the fire in and then raked it out and put the bread in. You can see where the one at Rowan Park was.'(2)

The house was abandoned and fell into decay, although the byres in the later portion were used by local farmers.

High Whelter Also known as Old Whelter, this building was a ruin in 1928. It was situated slightly higher and south of Low Whelter and it was possibly the original house in the settlement. The Hearth Tax 1669-1772 records no less than twelve houses or cottages in the Whelter area, eight householders were paying this tax and four were exempted. High or Old Whelter was absorbed into Low Whelter, probably in the early 19th century.

Low Whelter *'The house is first mentioned in the Church Registers in 1644 and was probably built not long before that date. In the 18thC an extension was built at the northern end and a further addition was made later. The house generally has been modernised. The interior has stop chamfered ceiling beams and exposed joists. A plain string between ground and first floors is carried along the E front.'*

On the top stone of the wall at Low Whelter there was a rough carving of a man's head with the date 1785 on it. Isaac Hinchliffe thought it to be of John Law, Bishop of Clonfert in Ireland, and the handiwork of Parson Hebson who lived at Whelter.

In 1789 Ann Radcliffe, an author and a contemporary of Jane Austin, visited the Lake District. She diverted from the main road at Shap, where she had stayed the night, and went to

Haweswater via Shap Abbey and Bampton. She describes her visit to Whelter, which she calls the Parsonage, as follows:

'The interior of the parsonage was as comfortable as the situation was interesting. A neat parlour opened from the passage, but it was newly painted, and we were shown into the family room, having a large old fashioned chimney corner, with benches to receive a social party, and forming a most enviable retreat from the storms of the mountains. The seat of a long window, overlooking the lake, offered the delights of other seasons; hence the luxuriance of summer and the colouring of autumn successively spread their enchantments over the opposite woods, and the meadows that margined the water below. And a little garden of sweets sent up its fragrance to that of the honeysuckles that twined round the window. The venerable father of the mansion was engaged at his chapel of Mardale but we were hospitably received within.'[3]

Latterly known only as Whelter, or Whelter Cottage, the house *'had more than a whiff of* the *Scandinavian about it'* according to David Hay who spent some childhood days there and described the house as follows:

'There were the long lofts that remained a feature of Lakeland farm houses long after other Scandinavian influences had disappeared. The Whelter upstairs was built on this principle but later partitioned and a steep stairway had replaced the ladder. The traditional oar had been built into the roof beams and outside the steading was protected from the evil spirits of the northern lands by a shield of sycamore trees.'[4]

In 1595, Henry Holme is recorded as living at Whelter though he may have been at High Whelter as that was the earlier dwelling. John and William Holme of Whelter were allocated seats in pews in Bampton church in 1726 and the family were last recorded there when William died in 1739. It is possible that this is the time when High Whelter was abandoned.

Before 1841 the Baxter, Winder, Harrison and Dennyson families lived here at various times. By the time of the 1841 census there was only one occupied dwelling, the tenants being Robert Richardson and his family. The Gilpin family were recorded as living here in the 1851 census, followed by Isaac Watson. In the 1891 census Robert Kitching and his wife,

Elizabeth, and family were living here. They moved to Sleagill, and in 1901 it was the home of Joseph and Elizabeth Mounsey and their sons. Low Whelter was finally joined with Flakehow for farming by the Edmondson family. Miss Hannah Edmondson ran the house as a bed and breakfast for a time.

The accommodation consisted of a kitchen, parlour, pantry and three bedrooms. Outside there was a barn, several loose boxes and a four stall byre with loft above.

Low Whelter

Slapestones - meaning slippery stones. This dwelling was probably built by one of the Holme family. In the last remaining building there was a slab inscribed GFH 1802.

The only entries in the church registers to name Slapestones show the following occupants:

22 October 1704	*Jane Holm of Slape Stone Spinster, buried*
13 December 1707	*William Holme of Slapestone, an old Batchelor buried*
29 November 1712	*William Holm of Slapestone married to Margaret Dennison of Bomby*
7 March 1719	*John son of William and Margaret Holme of Slape Stone*

Mardale Vicarage Before the vicarage was built in 1857, the vicars of Mardale had lived at Measand Grammar School, claimed their ancient rights to 'Whittlegate' or, as in the case of Parson Hebson, lived in one of the existing houses. The new Vicarage was built in 1857 under Castle Cragg by the Revd Thomas Holme.

Mardale Vicarage

RIGGINDALE

This name means valley of the ridge or *'rigg'* and was the area at the mouth of the great valley by the Rigg. It was another ancient settlement, which grew up around a great medieval field. Farms in this settlement included Flakehow, Riggindale Farm and Bowderthwaite.

Flakehow The name is derived from old Icelandic word *'fleikre'* meaning hurdle or wall and *'how'* meaning side of a hill.

'A mid 17thC farmhouse with a late 17thC addition at the N end and a modern extension N of the staircase wing. The interior has cambered and stop chamfered ceiling beams and stop chamfered joists. The kitchen has a fixed cupboard with moulded panels and is inscribed AH 1675 (for Holme). By the fireplace is a panelled 'spice Cupboard' of 17thC date and there is a circular brick lined oven.'

Flakehow was one of the larger farms in the valley with a seventeenth century farmhouse which survived into the 20th century. At least one or two earlier smaller farmsteads would have existed at Flakehow but would have been absorbed into the seventeenth century holding. In 1660 the customary tenants at 'Flackhow' were a Holme and a Dennison. The Holme family had a long association with Flakehow which probably began long before. The first definite record of the Holme family here was in 1659, and in 1680 when George Holme was in occupation. In 1726 Henry Holme Snr of Flakehow was allocated two seats in pew 10 and Henry Holme Jnr was allocated two seats in pew 10 in the church at Bampton.

Other names associated with Flakehow during these years are Bowman, Dennison, Dawes, Ion, Jackson and Atkinson.

John Bland and his family were in occupation at the time of the 1841 and 1851 censuses. In 1861 the Fishwick family lived here and farmed 90 acres. The 1871 census records Richard Martindale as farming 156 acres. Richard Martindale was again recorded here in the 1881 census. The Martindales were followed into Flakehow by the Edmondson family who stayed there until the valley was flooded. The last occupiers were Maggie Edmondson and her husband Jack Lancaster.

Riggindale Farm

'The western half of the house, together with the staircase wing on

Flakehow

Flakehow showing Castle Crag behind

the N Side is of mid 17thC date. Later in the century the house was extended eastwards. In the 18thC a one storey addition was built in the angle between the staircase and the S wings. The doors and windows have been rebuilt. The interior has stop chamfered and cambered beams. Condition poor.'

Helena Baily recalled that *'Riggindale House ...... overflows with noise and chatter and good food. It overflows with children too at times, they pour out of the doors and trickle out into neighbouring fields and becks. Some flow up and over the hills. Water flows there too, in at the roof and out of the butt onto the scullery floor.'*(5)

Built at the mouth of Riggindale the seventeenth century dwelling, like Flakehow, would have comprised at least two smaller dwellings sharing a Great Field. In a room in the house there was a cupboard dated 1674, the date of the rebuilding of the house which became known as Riggindale Farm.

In 1660 the customary tenants were two Hatons and a Browne. These families were also recorded as being here in the Bampton Church registers for 1677 and 1694. Riggindale was also associated with the Holme family who were recorded there in 1699, 1700, 1703, 1706 and 1711. The name of Greenhow appears here in 1779 and 1841, and in 1851 Thomas Greenhow and his family lived here. It was unoccupied at the time of the 1861 census. In 1871 George Brunskill was farming 336 acres at Riggindale. William Greenhow and his wife Elizabeth lived there in 1881 continuing the Greenhows long association with Riggindale. In 1891 John Howell was farming here but in 1901 William Greenhow had returned.

Riggindale

Bowderthwaite This name means an area cleared of boulders.

'The building is of later 17thC date, the eastern wing originally being a dwelling house. The first floor to this wing has been removed. There is an original two light window in the S. wall with chamfered jambs and mullion. The roof has curved struts to the tie beams and side purlins. The gables are crow stepped. Condition poor.'

The dwelling was situated on the southern flanks of Riggindale, and was reputed to be the first stone house built in Mardale. It was close to the site of Hugh Holme's cave in Riggindale and it is possible that he would have chosen this site for a dwelling on his emergence from 'hiding'. Bowderthwaite was an example of the need for protection from the weather and from passers-by of various types (Mardale was not always a vale of tranquillity!). The dwelling had tiny windows about 15 by 18 inches with very strong masonry, in spite of being built without mortar. It was probably absorbed into Chapel Hill in the late 1780s and had been used as an outbuilding for many years. The names of John Holme 1820, R M 1856, H P H (Hugh Parker Holme), T W 1814 (The Reverend. Thomas Wharton) and Richard Martindale 1851 were cut into the plaster inside. The only records in the church registers are

Bowderthwaite

those of the burial of Myles Holme of Bowderthwaite in 1707, and Myles Holme in 1737. Thomas Thompson, son of Edmund Thompson, was born here in 1740.

MARDALE GREEN

was the area at the head of the valley which comprised the original estate of the Holme family. Chapel Hill was for many centuries the dwelling place of the senior family of the Holmes, the Kings of Mardale. In 1660 the customary tenants were listed as Mr Robert Strickland, five by the name of Holme, a Jackson and a Bowman. The farms included in this settlement included Dudderridge Bank, Brackenhowe, Greenhead, Grove Brae (South Fold), Goosemire (North Fold), Chapel Hill, Field Head, Bowderthwaite, Garth Beck and Riggindale.

Field House *'The original structure was rectangular and of early to mid 17thC date. About 1700 the roof was carried down over additions at the W end of the S wall and the E end of the N. Wall. A portion of the S wall was cut away to open into the new SW addition. In the 18thC the western end of the N. wall was removed, and an addition built at that end. The portion of the wall which was removed being rebuilt a few feet further S. The original roof is in four bays and has four crutch trusses springing from half the height of the walls. The trusses have been cut about somewhat, but one of them retains the original collar. The main timbers were stop chamfered. The gable ends are crow stepped. Condition fair.'*

Field House lay behind and to the east of Chapel Hill. In spite of all the alterations and additions there is no mention of it in the church registers. It was absorbed into the Chapel Hill Estate.

Chapel Hill *'The four buildings are of 17thC date; they have all been dwelling-houses but are now used as barns. At the time of investigation they were hay-filled and their interiors were not therefore completely examined. One has been much altered, re-roofed etc. but retains its 17thC spinning gallery at the NW end. One is also much altered, but retains a few stop-chamfered ceiling beams and has remains in the NW gable, of a projecting chimney built out on wooden corbels. One is now ruinous its wall standing only 5-6ft. high; it* *consist of a 17thC ingle-nook with fire window and large chimney; the stack of the latter has a projection of 4ft. A smaller building has old chamfered roof timbers, crow step gables and a chimney built out on wooden corbels.'*

Behind the house built by Richard and Ann Holme in 1814 there were four earlier buildings. Chapel Hill took its name from the ancient chantry, and was in continuous use by the main branch of the Holmes family from medieval times until the death of Hugh Parker Holme in 1885. The estate which grew around it included many of the small holdings including Goosemire, Grove Brae, Brackenhowe, Field House, Bowderthwaite and the Dun Bull, or Greenhead as it was formerly known.

After the death of the last of the line, Hugh Parker Holme, it was occupied by James C Bowstead, his brother in law in 1891. John Hudson was the tenant in 1901 and 1911. The Jacksons also lived at Chapel Hill for many years, probably as shepherds in the service of the Holme family.

Brackenhowe *'A 17thC farmhouse with early 18thC additions at the N and S ends, that at the south end being a barn. Between ground and first floors is a plain string of slates. The interior has stop chamfered ceiling beams and exposed joists. Condition poor.'*

Brackenhowe was the highest house in Mardale and lay on the western side of Mardale Green under the Craggs. Another dwelling called Dudderwicke or Dudderigg Bank lay in the vicinity of Brackenhowe. Two children were born to Thomas Holme in 1679 and 1680. Here, however, the name never appears after 1698 when it is recorded that *'Barbary Holme of Duddrigge dyed'*. The holding may have been absorbed into Brackenhowe and the house abandoned. Dodderwick Force descends from the crags in this area.

While the later house dates from the seventeenth century, it is obvious from the registers that there was a dwelling here as

Chapel Hill

Brackenhowe

early as 1597. The house also has early 18th century additions. The first mention of Brackenhowe in the Shap church registers is the baptism of *'Isabell Haton, dt* (daughter) *to John of Brackenhowe'* in 1597. Ezabell Holme ,daughter, to John of *'Breckenhowe'*, was baptised in 1613, and Thomas Holme died here in 1707.

Brackenhowe was absorbed into the Chapel Hill Estate and the house used for farm servants, although it was often unoccupied. The 1881 census records William and Elizabeth Greenhow living here with their family.

Greenhead with the Dun Bull on the right

Greenhead This house was unique and set apart in its architecture from the limestone rendered farmhouses traditional in the valley as it was built of dark green Mardale/Westmorland slate and left un-rendered.

Mrs Elizabeth Holme, the widow of the Reverend Thomas Holme, built the house known locally as 'The Mansion' after the death of her husband, as she had to leave the Vicarage. The site by the Dun Bull was chosen as the land was already owned by the Holme family. She lived at The Mansion with a companion, and her staff, for much of the year but as she became older she spent time at Patterdale Vicarage with her niece, where she died. (More details of Elizabeth Holme's life can be found in Chapter 5). The Mansion was absorbed into the Dun Bull after her death.

Goosemire (North Fold)

'A small farmhouse of the later half of the 17thC, with an 18thC extension at the S end. The doorway is fitted with a studded door of 17thC date. The interior has stop chamfered ceiling beams and exposed joists and has a wooden partition with moulded vertical boarding. The first floor has been entirely modernised and the roof ceiled. About 50 yds SE of the house is a later

17thC barn of rubble with a roof of stone slates. It is two storyed and has crow stepped gables at the N and S ends. The roof is in three bays and has stop chamfered tie beams. Condition good.'

Helena Baily recalls that:

'Goosemire was a typical Lake District farmhouse though rather smaller than some. It was built of local stone, the walls were some 2ft thick, with a roof of local slate. The front only was plastered and whitewashed, though most other houses were whitewashed all round. Attached to the house were the buildings, wash house with loft above and at right angles the stables and hay loft and beyond that the earth closet. There were shippons across the track with a secluded garden behind for vegetables and raspberries and currant bushes. Further down the track towards the lake there was a big hay barn. The house faced east towards the fellside so we didn't get much sun. The water supply was an iron spout out of the fellside into a wooden tub some 50 yards across the track. That bit of fell was an 'inta'k which you entered at the bottom or left at the top of the' ootgang'. It was called the Girsings, where a flock of geese were kept in the old days, and this, together with the boggy nature of the ground round the water supply, probably gave the house its name.

Before you entered the house there was a stone slab on the right about waist high; which was useful for washing up and other odd jobs on a fine day, with a small triangular garden behind it which was not much use except for its supply of raspberries, as the only way in was to climb over the wall behind the slab. The house was entered by a porch about six feet deep with a stone slab about knee height on the right, used for water buckets on top and dirty boots below.

The door opened straight on to the big kitchen with the staircase running straight up ahead. To the left was a small parlour which Cousin Gwendolen used as a bedroom and sanctum. On the right hand wall facing the garden there were two quite large windows with deep windowsills in the thickness of the wall, quite wide enough to tuck yourself into comfortably with a book.

Tucked into the corner of the next wall, quite high up was the hen cupboard, with a beautifully carved oak door, so-called because the hen meal was kept there, though we used it for dry goods. The main feature of that wall however, taking up the centre half space was the enormous black kitchen range, reaching the height of a man, with a mantel shelf on top which traditionally stood a clock and treasured ornaments safely out of the way.

The square fire-box in the centre was protected by several iron bars, from the bottom of which stuck out an iron trivet on which could be balanced a saucepan or flat irons for heating. There was a big ash box below. To the left of the fire was the water boiler with a lid on top and tap near the bottom for withdrawal of the hot water. To the right was the hot oven, with the cool oven below. Above the fire an iron bar stuck out on a pivot so that it could be swung about. From the end hung a bar ending with a hook which could be adjusted in height by holes, from which hung an iron kettle or pan over the fire.

To the right of the stove was the coal scuttle and wood box and to the left the hay box.

In the corner of the next room was the hen window, so called because you could keep an eye on the hens in the field. (We didn't have any hens!) The rest of the wall was taken up by traditional oak dresser with china and against the staircase wall our old toy cupboard for books and so on.

In the corner under the stairs was the dairy-cum-pantry with big stone slabs and a small window. Here was kept the food and a large assortment of pots and pans.

Upstairs the bedroom to the left was traditionally the men's room and here slept my brothers and their friends. To the right a narrow landing led past the master bedroom where mother and father slept, to the girl's room. This arrangement in farming days was so that the master and mistress could hear if any of the men tried to slip past them to the girl's room.'[6]

Goosemire was formerly known as North Fold. It was situated on the same side of the valley as Grove Brae and at about the same elevation, so it fits the description of the 'North Fold'. In the Baily records there is mention that Goosemire was altered in the early 1900s and during that time the family lived in the old cottage by the sheep yard. This may have been the pre 17th century cottage known as North Fold. There is no mention in the records of Goosemire until the 1881 census; however, in the RCHME survey of 1935 it is described as a seventeenth century house.

Grove Brae (South Fold)

'The House is of late 17thC date with later 18thC extensions to S. The ingle-nook was at the S.end. It has a spice cupboard inscribed with date and initials WEH 1682. There are stop chamfered ceiling beams and chamfered joists. Windows and chimneys are modern.'

Grove Brae was known as the Southfold in early times. The dwelling nestled at the foot of the fell under the confluence of Rowantreethwaite and Hopghyll becks on the eastern side of Mardale Green. It was probably built by William and Elizabeth Holme. The house had a kitchen, scullery and pantry with three bedrooms and a lumber room. Outside there was a good range of buildings including a twelve stall byre, a six stall byre, a stable, seven loose boxes, and a calf box, all with lofts. A barn, cart shed and a pig hull completed the holding.

In 1714 Elizabeth, daughter to William Holme, was born here followed by another daughter, Agnes, in 1717. In 1728, Henry, son of John and Janet Turner, was born here. In 1730, John, the son of John and Janet, died and was the first person to be buried in the new burial ground at Mardale Church.

Grove Brae was the home of the Mawson family for many years, beginning with Aaron Mawson recorded there in the 1841 census until 1875. Robert Clark and his family were in residence in 1881. They were also providing lodging for a group of tradesmen, masons, plasterers and painters who were building the house for Mrs Elizabeth Holme. In 1891 John Irving, a shepherd, was living there with his wife and four small daughters. Thomas Watson appeared as the farmer of 60 acres there in 1901 and 1911. The Bell family were the last tenants at Grove Brae.

Garth Beck (or Garth End)

There was very little trace of Garth Beck although it appeared many times in records and documents. There were the remains of a house near Arnold Bridge, close by a great sycamore, which was identified as the site. The Holmes were

Goosemire

Grove Brae

recorded here in 1734 and 1735, with an entry for Haiton (Hayton) in 1771. Garth Beck probably was an ancient building predating the late 17th century rebuild and which gradually fell out of use.

GUERNESS (GIRNISHE)

'My favourite place is Guerness, on the shore of the lake. It has a nice sandy beach where we can build castles and harbours for Dick's ships. We make roads there too. It is a lovely place for bathing. At first when you go bathing it is stony, but soon it is nice and soft. You can go out a long way before the water comes up to your neck. You get to it by a cart track, then a path through the wood.'[7]

Guerness was an ancient place with the remnants of an ancient settlement. The name appears in the registers in 1594 when Agnes, daughter to Willim Jackson of Girnishe, was baptised, followed in 1595 with the burial of William's son, Henry. William would have been from the same family who occupied Naddle at this time. The Bowman family were recorded here in 1687. There were also remains of dwellings on the shoreline near Guerness Nib.

Higher up Guerness Ghyll there was a charcoal burners' settlement which had developed to the extent that it had a beer house and a mill. Copper was worked at Guerness for some years between 1836 and 1852 but not in any great amounts. There are still traces of the industry on the site, which was cut through by the building of the 'new road'.

Chapter 5

Mardale Chapel

The Chapel sat in perfect rural seclusion by the roadside leading to Mardale Green, against a background of the mountains which grew out of the head of Mardale. Its origins are shrouded in legend and Joseph Whiteside finally commented that 'all we know for certain is that there was a chapel before 1700.' He left the question open to reasonable argument by stating 'there is no inherent impossibility in the planting of a chapel before 1400.'(1)

It is not known when Christianity came to the valley. Joseph Whiteside, the vicar of Shap 1897-1900, in his book 'Shappe in Bygone Days' suggested that the successors of the peoples who first occupied the ancient place may have heard stories of the 'one true and only God, who had sent His Son to regenerate the world' from the 'tourists and commercial travellers' who followed the Roman legionnaries along High Street. These travellers may have ventured down into the valley to seek refreshment or to trade their merchandise. Stories of far off lands across the sea would be told whilst they traded with the local people. We may assume that, from these very early stories and the influence and teachings of the early Celtic missionaries, Christianity took root and became more established among the people of the dale as they gradually gave up their pagan Gods. Even then, some of the customs and traditions of the pre-Christian era prevailed until the end of the occupation of Mardale.

The yew trees which grew around the Chapel were very old, 700 to 800 years according to some opinions. However yew trees are difficult to date as much depends on soil and climate. Legend has it that the Kendal Bowmen used branches from them to make their bows which would have made them very ancient. It is probably safer to assume that they were planted in 1727 when the Chapel underwent extensive reordering and the graveyard was created. This theory is verified by Joseph

Two views of Mardale Church

Whiteside who was told by Mr W Jameson, the engineer in charge of the Haweswater Dam project, that the yearly growth rings on the trunk of the largest tree were counted after it was felled and that the number came to 187.

Joseph Whiteside describes a petition written in Latin, and found in the church chest, which was sent to the Bishop of Carlisle in 1728. This refers to the undoubted existence of a chapel *'which has been used from time immemorial'*[(2)] Joseph

Whiteside also referred to a document, loaned to him by Mrs Holme, the widow of the Reverend Thomas Holme, which stated that *'in the fourteenth century Rudolphus Holme founded an oratory or house of prayer near his habitation which took its name from that.'*[3] The dwelling referred to here was Chapel Hill. In spite of Joseph Whiteside's reluctance to confirm the existence of a place of worship from such early times, we can assume with some certainty that there was one, as whenever mankind settled in a new place he created a sacred place to his Gods, second only in importance to his own shelter and the provision of food. The Parish registers of Shap support the existence of an earlier chapel in the following entries:

Buried Maie xxx 1594 Sir Tomas Watson curat of M'dall
(Thomas Watson and Elizabeth Holme of Mardall had been married in August 1583)
Buried July xviii 1597 Agnes Holme dt to robert layt Reder of M'dall
Buried August vi 1600 Randall Brockbank Reder at Mardall and sonne to Sr John Brockbank vicar
of this pish of Shapp.

On 24th November 1663 a licence to teach school and read prayers was granted to Edward Stephenson.

The ecclesiastical boundaries of Mardale were not as well defined as those of the Manor, and later, the Parish boundaries; however, the whole valley was served by the Chapel at one time or another. The ancient designation of Chapel rather than Church persisted because for much of its early existence it was only a place of worship, or Chapel of Ease, and enjoyed none of the privileges of a Parish Church, which were provided by St Michael's Church at Shap, or for those at the north and west side of the valley, St Patrick's at Bampton.

Until 1728 all baptisms, marriages and burials took place in the two mother churches. The residents from the part of the valley in Shap Parish sometimes attended Bampton during the winter months, as there are entries in the Bampton registers indicating that this would have been the easier option. The Corpse Road, as it is still known, wound its way east to Shap, initially by a very steep climb by Hopgill Beck over Swindale Common and down to Swindale Head, then by Tailbert, Keld and on to St Michael's Church at Shap seven miles away. This route would be impossible to travel in times of heavy snow, especially when transporting a coffin for burial or a new born child for a baptism.

By the early 1700s the residents of Mardale tired of the trek to Shap and Bampton and in 1728, shortly after the new Church at Bampton was consecrated, they sent a petition to the Bishop of Carlisle.[4] To substantiate their plea they cited the following:

'The great distance from their Parish Churches which causes excessive expense for funerals and the souls as well as the bodies of infants taken to be baptized are endangered. To receive the sacraments, as befits sons of Holy Church, it is impossible without much toil and inconvenience, especially in the snows and floods of winter. They have no doubt about the consecration of the chapel, which has been used from time immemorial. They pay the curate reasonable fees and emoluments, as in the neighbouring chapelries. The chapel is well-roofed and in proper repair.

They undertake for themselves and their heirs to respect the rights and privileges of Shap and Bampton vicars, and to go on supporting a curate of their own. They humbly implore the bishop to grant a licence for burials, baptisms, marriages and any other rites of the church. No obstacle is raised by Edmund Noble, Minister of Shap or Thomas Wearing, vicar of Bampton.'

The Bishop agreed to the request and permission, with various conditions relating to the rights of the Vicars of Shap and Bampton, and a financial commitment to their minister, was signed and sealed on 15th July 1728. At this point the description of 'Church' could be applied to the building. No dedication can be proved but it was often described as All Saints Church. The first burial carried out at Mardale was that of John Turner, son of John Turner (by his first wife), of the Fold in 1731.

Old ties were hard to break and for many years after 1728 the entries in the Mardale register were duplicated in the Shap register. Families who had formed allegiances with the two parish churches just before the licensing of the Chapel continued the habit, in one or two cases to reunite couples separated by death for example 'June 7th 1736 John Holme of Brackenhowe, the last corps carried from Mardale to be buried at Shap.'[4] Those who lived at Measand and the foot of the valley continued to attend Bampton Church.

What of the Church which we know from photographs, the one which was demolished when the Haweswater Reservoir was created? There are various opinions as to when it was first built. It was obviously not the original sanctuary of Rudolphus Holme, although it is likely that it was built on the same site. Noted Victorian antiquarians such as W G Collingwood were of the opinion that the building dated from the seventeenth century. Isaac Hinchcliffe, the author of 'Backwater in Lakeland' stated that *'The present church was built towards the end of the seventeenth century, and probably replaced a more primitive building.'*[5]

In their survey of Westmorland, dated 1935, the RCHME[6] decided that the roof of the building was late medieval and therefore that the main structure was 'probably of medieval date' with a West Tower added in 1737, the time of the petition to the Bishop of Carlisle. From a document dated 1737 and reproduced below it can be seen that a great deal of work was done to the building at that time, indicating that this was the substantial refurbishment of an existing building. How much rebuilding was done and whether it included the building of a tower is not clear, but the work was extensive as there is mention of the glazing of the windows and this may have included new windows. It is interesting to note that the work was completed using local resources for material and manpower. All the people mentioned in the document lived in the valley or the near neighbourhood.

**spikins are small pieces of sheep's bones used for fixing slates etc.*

Joseph Whiteside had the best opportunity to make an archaeological assessment of the Church as he was a historian as well as a clergyman and had a great interest in the history of his parish, particularly Mardale. He described the building as follows:

An Account of the Money got by Collection, Benifaction & Assesment towards the rebuilding of Mardale Chappel, as also the disburstments of the Same. 1737

Money received.

	£ s d
Collection & Benifaction money	8:16:1
Mr Holmes & Mr Lancasters Gift	6:6:0
John Summers Benifaction	0:10:0
Received for goods bought at sale	1:5:4 ¾
Money borrow'd of ye Chappelstock	7:14:0
Receiv'd by an Assesment	15:5:8
Rec'd in all	39:17:1 ¾

Disburstments.

To Wm Lowis for work	0:16:8
To Thos Dixon for work	3:15:0
To Edmund Jon for work	3:19:0
To John Lancaster for lime	2:11:6
To Robert Willson for Slate	2:14:0
To Jeremiah Smith for freestone	2:13:0
To Wm Sinclar for Spiking	0:0:6
To Robt Briggs for Spikins	0:1:6
for Latts & Nails	0:12:1

Extract from accounts for the rebuilding of Mardale Chapel, 1737

'The interior measurements of the fabric are: Length 31 feet; width 16 feet 6 inches. The height of the tower is 29 feet 6 inches; its width, 10 feet three inches. The font was the gift in June 1872 of Mary Elizabeth, wife of the Rev. Thomas Holme, in memory of her mother, the pulpit came from Crosby Ravensworth; the oak of its predecessor now panels the walls under the seats of the chancel which is separated from the rest of the chapel by a neat oak screen. This, with the semi circular altar and surrounding rails, may be assigned to the year 1737, a date painted on the central panel of the gallery.'[7]

Whiteside was certain *'the tower is quite modern and built against the fabric, that the bell is dated 1825* and that there is a trace of a disused doorway in the south wall, which would be closed when the tower was erected. The two benches in the gallery may be the last survivors of the original seats; they were clumsy and rough made at home of Mardale oak, but have recently undergone some restoration.*

The windows on either side are plain, narrow and round-headed, three feet high and with wide splays. They appear to be coeval with the walls, except the east window which was inserted in 1860 taking the place of a two light of the same style as the others. Above it is a scroll 'Let all thy works praise Thee', and above the altar, verse 34 of chapter xiii of St John's Gospel with the monogram I H S.

The massive axe hewn beams of native oak in the roof are noticeable; the walls, too, are of considerable thickness.'

*This could possibly also be the date that the tower was built.

The weather vane on the tower was given by John Holme of Chapel Hill to commemorate the birth of his daughter, Ann Marie, in 1842.

Any further possibility of investigating the age of the Chapel disappeared when it was demolished.

The earliest people to minister in Mardale would almost certainly be the canons from Shap Abbey. The Abbey had taken over the rectory of St Michael's at Shap in 1200 and from then, until the dissolution, church services were led by various canons. As Mardale was a Chapel of St Michael's the same arrangement would have applied. It is possible that it was canons from Shap Abbey who persuaded Rudolphus Holme to provide land and money to build that very early place of worship, reputed to date from 1350. The record of various readers and curates assigned to Mardale go back to 1594 but from January 1540, when the end came for Shap Abbey, until 1594, Mardale would have been served by those who filled the place of the canons after the dissolution of the Abbey.

From those early times until 1842 the Minister of the Chapel was also the master at the School. The first record of someone in this dual roll was 1663 when Edward Stephenson was licensed to teach at the school and read prayers. This appointment indicated that that there was some form of education prior to the endowment of the Grammar School at Measand 1711. Edward Stephenson probably taught pupils in the Chapel. There would have been nothing unusual with this; before the boys' school was endowed at Shap in 1835, boys were taught in St Michael's Church.

From the Diocesan Registry the following list of readers, curates and incumbents was preceded by the four names found in the Shap Registers dating from 1594.

Church interior showing the gallery

The pulpit and sanctuary

1703 Michael Sommers *
1708 William Langhorn *
1722 Jonathan Tinclar *
1723 William Robinson *
1726 Thomas Baxter *
1731 Richard Holme
1734 William Collinson *
1739 John Watson *
1741 Bartholomew Hayes *
1749 Richard Hebson *
1800 John Bowstead *
1842 John Rowlandson (Vicar of Shap)
1858 Thomas Holme M.A.
1880 Henry Wilkinson Scaife. M.A
1882 Charles Henry Hatfield, M.A.
1882 Arthur Anderson Williams M.A.
1885 Charles Newton Greenwood M.A
1891 Hugh Charles Baldwin B.A
1894 William Terry
1918 Frederick H.J. Barham.

* These Vicars were also Masters of the Grammar School at Measand.

Some of the clergy are worthy of particular note. Thomas Baxter and Richard Holme were from local families and would have received their schooling at Measand Grammar School.

Richard Hebson (1749) was Vicar and Master for 51 years. He lived at Whelter and in his declining years he was assisted by vicars from nearby Parishes. In the Shap Church accounts for 1795 there is an amount for 3s 6d for 'the vicar's Easter dinner at Mardale'. This vicar was James Holme who had journeyed over to Mardale to take the Easter service.

John Bowstead (1800) held the posts of Vicar and Master for 42 years. He was born at Great Salkeld and married Peggy Mounsey of Eastward, Bampton. They had seven children. He took took part wholeheartedly in the life of the dale and is mentioned as a major participant in a song, called 'The Askham Harriers', the words of which appeared in the Cumberland and

Sketch of Mardale church by Thomas Bland

Westmorland Advertiser. The song gives an account of the hunt for a legendary hare. He was fondly known as 'auld Boosty' and there is a well known picture of him in Bampton Church Hall. Included in the picture is a lancet with a tortoise-shell shaft which he used to bleed the Mardale congregation. By the end of March they would remind him that it was about time he 'brout t' lancet.' On the following Sunday the congregation would move to Chapel Hill where the whole company was bled in the arm. Today it is hard to imagine what benefit this operation would have had, or the side effects. However in those days 'letting blood' was believed to be an essential annual spring clean for the system.

Joseph Whiteside said of him *'It would not be easy to find a score of parish priests in any diocese with half the classical attainments of Bowstead, and it's a shame that such a man should have received no ecclesiastical reward. He was a capital preacher with a fine flow of language. He is said to have talked in the dialect but this is not perfectly accurate. With farmers and with friends he used the vernacular, as some of us do still but in church and school he spoke the King's English.'*[8]

Bowstead was assisted in his work by two Greenhow brothers. Described as curates, they were Mardale men, the sons of John and Mary Greenhow, and would probably have been tutored by Richard Hebson at the Grammar School. One of them, William, was recorded as carrying out a baptism in 1824. Sadly his death occurred one year later when the burial of the Reverend William Greenhow, age 25, was recorded. His brother, John Greenhow, was still assisting in 1834. John Bowstead's incumbency ended with his death in 1842, when the joint position of Vicar and Master also ceased.

John Bowstead was succeeded by the Reverend James Rowlandson, who had been the Vicar of Shap since 1819. At various times he had the assistance of curates at Mardale. Rowlandson had received his early schooling at Bampton Grammar School and although he was only incumbent of Mardale for eleven years he was held in high esteem. He drove over to Mardale on Sunday afternoons, not an easy task for an ageing man with twelve gates to open between Bomby and

Mardale, and three in the Abbey Grange. One of his last duties carried out at the Chapel was the baptism of James Joseph, son of John and Mary Holme of Chapel Hill.

Thomas Holme (1858) was the son of Richard Holme of Chapel Hill. He was the younger brother of John and uncle to Hugh Parker Holme. Like Rowlandson, he received his early schooling at Bampton Grammar School. After gaining his MA at Queens College, Oxford he was curate in charge of Emmanuel Church, Loughborough, under the founder, his uncle the Reverend William Holme BD, a native of Mardale. He moved to the Rectory of Puttenham in Hertfordshire in 1849. In 1850 he married Miss Mary Elizabeth Croshar, daughter of the Church Warden at Loughborough. They left Puttenham in 1858, when Thomas took up the living at Mardale.

'Aided by his brothers and sisters, he built the parsonage and made it over to the living. He also restored the church with the help of his relations and the Earl of Lonsdale. He was a zealous promoter of every improvement in the neighbourhood and endeared himself to all around him by his courteous, upright and peace loving example.'[9]

Following Thomas Holme there were five appointments in quick succession. However these men were obviously not enamoured of life in this remote dale as their incumbencies were short. They obviously had none of the qualities of endurance of those who went before, or came after them. Charles Henry Hatfield resigned before he took up his position. He must have taken the job, site unseen, and when he saw the dale he fled.

In 1894 William Terry, known as Terry of Mardale, was appointed. He bonded closely with the people of Mardale and under his ministry the Church prospered. Joseph Whiteside said of him

'He remains a model to the fell side Clergy whose lot is cast in very lonely and difficult surroundings.'[10]

Much is known of the life in the valley, particularly the Church, and of the energy that both the Revd and Mrs Sarah Terry devoted to the parish, from reports included in the deanery magazine for this period.

Mrs Elizabeth Holme, the widow of the Reverend Thomas Holme, figured largely in the life of the Church and supported it generously, both financially and practically. She paid for the heating and lighting of the Church for many years and also took part in the annual concert and dance playing duets with Miss Barrow, her niece and companion. She also held sway in other areas. One story told was that if she did not approve of a hymn when it was announced she would halt the proceedings and choose one of her own. Many of the visitors to the valley read lessons at the services on Sundays. Extracts from the magazine illustrate the extent of the support for the Terry family from all the families in the valley. Most of the events held, whatever their nature, were manned by Kitchings, Edmondsons, Greenhows, Hudsons, Mounseys and Baldrys. Messrs Edmondson, Hudson and Greenhow all served as Church wardens at some point. There is little record of the life of the Church before 1894 when these articles were published, but some events must have been established before this and were enhanced and added to by the Terry's.

The Sunday School was well attended, usually by about twenty children. During the year there were several special celebrations. In January there was the annual prize giving. On one of these occasions the books were presented by Mrs Terry and the Vicar gave a lecture entitled 'Round the world in 60 minutes' with lantern slides. Oranges and cakes were supplied by Mrs Holme. At Christmas there was a big party with special treats, usually funded by Mrs Holme, and another party took place in late summer when a picnic was held either on the Rigg or in the woods by Guerness.

Wharton Bibles and Prayer Books were presented annually to all children *'who shall be taught to and be able to say, by heart, the Catechism, some ofthe Prayers according to the Church of England as well as the 1st, 15th, 25th, 101st, 113th and 145th Psalms.'*[11]

The annual flower service was held in mid July. This was an open air service for children and young people and took place in the Churchyard by the yew trees. After the service the flowers brought to the service were firstly placed in the Church and, after the evening service, on the graves. In the early days of this event the collection was given in eggs. On some occasions as many as 104 were given and distributed among the residents at Shap Workhouse, Penrith Cottage Hospital or the needy in the Parish. Latterly money was given and used for the benefit of the choir.

Another annual event was the choir trip. A long day was spent travelling by train to Blackpool or Morecambe. One year the venue was the Royal Show at Carlisle and another year a trip to Keswick. At one point there must have been signs that the main reason for membership of the choir was the chance of being eligible for the Choir trip which was usually held jointly with Bampton Church. A rule was introduced making it necessary for those wishing to make the trip to attend at least two thirds of choir practices. Apparently numbers on ensuing trips were somewhat decimated. Again these events were financed to a large degree by the generosity of Mrs Holme.

The major festivals of the Church were fully celebrated. Advent services led up to Christmastide and a Watch-night service was always held on New Years' Eve. Two services were held on Good Friday and four on Easter Sunday. Much effort was put into filling the Church with suitable floral decorations on these occasions. At Harvest Festival time flowers were often sent from Lowther Castle to use in the Church and Mr Hudson had a model of a Dutch barn which was used in the displays for many years.

The parishioners willingly met all requests for items for the Church. In 1899 it was decided to replace the harmonium which had done service for 30 or more years. An organ fund was started with a donation of £5 and an American organ was installed at a cost of £20. Lists of items wanted appeared in the magazine under the heading *'We are always wanting!'* Items included bookmarkers for the Church Bible, a smaller Prayer Book and a set of copies of Hymns Ancient and Modern for use by the choir, to mention but a few.

In the same year thanks were recorded again to Mrs Holme who with Miss Barrow *'procured a complete set of hassocks which will be a great improvement, both as to comfort and appearance upon the rough wooden blocks which have done duty for so many years.'* On another occasion it is recorded that new curtains were provided for the vestry and a new bell rope in the tower. The

Measand Mission was held for many years in the kitchen at Measand Beck Farm, usually mid week during the summer. Whether this was held by another denomination is not clear but there was certainly a link with the Church as there are several reports of the meetings in the Ruridecanal Magazine.

Sadness came to the Terry family when Sarah Terry died at Mardale Vicarage in 1906, after being ill for several years. She was survived by her husband, four daughters and a son. The flag on the church tower flew at half mast from the Tuesday when she died, until her burial on the Thursday *'a constant reminder of the sorrow which had fallen on the parish.'*[12] The sadness of the occasion was all the more poignant as her only son, a marine engineer, was on a ship bound for Bombay at the time of her death. William Terry left Mardale in 1910 and took up the living of Waverton cum Dundraw near Wigton where he served for twenty one years. He did marry again, but when he died in 1935 he was laid to rest with Sarah, who had been buried at Bampton.

In a tribute written to him in the local newspaper, Joseph Whiteside recalled their long friendship, having served with him as a young curate at West Hartlepool. He recalled that *'Terry had a very broad native Knarsdale accent and that his vowels were scarcely up to the accepted standard.'*

He went on to say *'When Mardale became vacant in 1894, as I thought some rest would benefit him (Terry) I asked my father (Stephen, then the Vicar of Shap) to offer him the benefice. There he remained for sixteen years, never dull or bored, with as many organizations as a large town, always occupied, with his printing machines and phonograph, making slides, and records, rushing all over the district in all weather to lecture, with lantern cylinder, poles and paraphernalia strapped on somehow to a venerable push-bike What a bundle of enthusiastic energy. In Westmorland he is still recalled with affectionate admiration and he remains a model to the fell side clergy whose lot is cast in very lonely and difficult surroundings.'*()

The last vicar of Mardale was the Reverend Frederick W Barham. By the time he took up the living at Mardale in 1911 the threat of the flood had begun to loom over the valley. He

The Reverend F H J Barham at the Church door

led a lonely existence at the Vicarage but was looked after by the few remaining families in the dale. There are many stories about his time in Mardale. It was not always possible to have an organist at services so he used a gramophone to play the hymns. No doubt that would add to the atmosphere as often

The last service

there were only a couple of people in the congregation. He probably looked forward to the summer holidays when there was a human injection in the form of the Baily family, particularly as Mrs Baily was an organist.

Helena Bailey remembers:

'But the person I really want to tell you about is the vicar, Mr Barham. He was the dearest, kindest most saintly old man. He was a bachelor, he lived in that enormous Victorian vicarage, he looked after himself and he was a real parish priest to the dale and to any visitors who came. Church was a very important part of our life, because we were Vicar's children and we were used to going to church, and the church was such a beautiful, warm, holy place; the sanctuary was all oak, and it was very curious, the altar table was semi-circular, so that the altar rail was semi-circular, which was nice because you were all round the Lord's table. Now we sat in what I imagine must have been the choir pews in the side of the sanctuary in cross pews which faced Mr Barham in his pulpit. That gave us a good view looking sideways of everyone in the congregation.

Now, inside the chancel was the harmonium and that was a splendid instrument with masses of stops and Maggie Edmondson, the youngest daughter from Flake How played the harmonium and I

The Reverend Barham with a parishioner

remember my sister and I were so envious of her because she was very pretty, We used to do the altar flowers and with luck we managed wild daffodils, for Easter and then in the summer we very often put bunches of wild flowers in. Sometimes Mr Barham used to give us a great treat and take us up the church tower and on top of the church roof so that we could survey our domain.

Every one has heard about the gramophone but I only ever heard Mr Barham use it once. It was a jolly sensible idea, if there was no-one to play the hymns, and you're an old clergyman and you've a motley collection of congregation, who was going to start the hymn up?

Mr Hinchcliffe (the person held responsible for the loss of the valley to Manchester) used to love to read the lessons. Mr Barham of course

Mardale Church by Caroline Crompton

The Harmonium

The Mardale Communion Plate

was on our side (against the building of the dam) and Mr Hinchcliffe one day got up to read the lesson and to our mystification he read a long chapter of the 'begats' – so and so begat so-and-so and all the terrible names which no one could pronounce anyway, and he got right to the end, and Mr Barham said, "I'm afraid that you have read the wrong lesson, now can we have the right one." There were many giggles from the Baily family.

Mr Edmondson the churchwarden would sit opposite us. He was a very large man and during the sermon he used to twiddle his thumbs round and round one way and then the other. We used to have bets on how many times he would twiddle one way or the other.'(13)

Mr Barham left Mardale in 1935. He returned for the final service but it is believed that he refused to sit inside with the numerous clergy and invited guests from near and far, and stood instead on the hill with the crowd.

The valley prospered for many hundreds of years with a settled population. Days of joy and sadness were marked with births and marriages. Most men and women looked very close to home when choosing a spouse. Very few families were left untouched by infant mortality or death due to the rigours of childbirth. Several families lost all their children from childhood diseases. Even so there were many examples of people living to a great age. The life of the valley revolved around these happenings and the Chapel was at the centre of it all.

Chapter 6

The Dun Bull

If the Church was the spiritual heart of the community, then the Dun Bull was its secular heart.

The earliest dwelling used as a hostelry was known as Greenhead. The first definite record of this dwelling occurs in the Shap church registers in 1686 when a son, William, was born to 'William Jackson 'oth Greenhead.' The Inn was also mentioned in a poem as early as 1772 when the landlord was Mr Jack Mounsey.[(1)] At a place on the track where refreshments and shelter would be needed, the farm, already brewing ale for its own use, gradually developed into an inn. Greenhead was originally a simple yeoman's farmhouse. Thomas Lamley, who took up the tenancy of Greenhead in 1825, responded to the increasing demand from tourism and built a large extension with a date stone, T L 1827. He was a man of humour, or maybe eccentricity, as he began to build a tower on Wood Howe so that he might see over into Swindale and Patterdale. This project came to nothing as the building only reached twenty feet. His other project of note was to make a wagon out of a hollowed out tree on wheels which he drove to Penrith on market day drawn by his horse, Dragon. This conveyance caused much amusement when it arrived in town.

Greenhead, or the Dun Bull Inn as it eventually became known, gained its reputation during the early years of Lake District tourism. The passes of Nanbield and Gatescarth were two of the established north-south routes and, for hundreds of years prior to the advent of the railway, travellers had come north over these passes and through the dale in large numbers.

In 1840 when Mr John Holme purchased the establishment an account of the festivities held was reported in the Westmorland Gazette[(2)] and gives a valuable insight into the customs at the time when the Dun Bull was first discovered by tourists.

'Mr Bowstead of Measand was chairman, supported by Mr Powley

Sketch of Mardale Green by J Sands (early 1840s). The artist's impression of the Dun Bull is on the right in the trees, Lamley's Tower can be seen on Wood Howe.

The Dun Bull

of Thrimby Grange. The King ordered a most liberal supply of punch, of which all partook enjoyably with much good humour. The health of Lord Lonsdale was received with the greatest enthusiasm and cheers oft repeated. Also of the host with three times three" Many toasts were drunk to absent Holmes, to Thomas Wharton and John Bowstead to Thomas Noble of High How, to Tinclar of Bomby and Taylor of Bald

How, the famous hunter who had brought his dogs for a few days sport. Matthew Betham of Towcet sang Around the Hugh Oak, the chairman the Sunny Hills and Mr Parker of Penrith the Blind Fiddler.'

The purchase of the Dun Bull by Mr John Holme brought it into the Chapel Hill Estate and the census of 1841 records William Towers as the publican although the name was still Greenhead. The first time the Inn is referred to as the Dun Bull is in the 1851 census when William Towers, Farmer and Innkeeper, was tenant there with his sister and nephew. The 1861 census records Joseph Bell as the Innkeeper, with his son-in-law, Joseph Airey, who farmed the forty acres attached to the Dun Bull.

A visitors' book[3] survives for the years from 1856 to 1862, and contains many interesting entries. The Inn was now called the 'Dun Bull Hotel' and was the haunt of fly fishers, fell walkers and day trippers. From the entries it is clear that these visitors came from far and wide, as well as local residents who took their guests for walks and trips on the lakes, taking either lunch or tea at the Dun Bull. Others were fell walkers who took various routes to the Hotel and wrote details of their walks in the book, and fishermen who boasted about the catches they had made. Visitors were not just from Great Britain. Mr Ridout from Toronto, Canada stayed in 1856. Mr Wilfred Lawson from Melbourne stayed in 1857, accompanied by Mr Kirkbride from Bampton. Other countries mentioned in the book include Spain, France and Portugal. On the 12th May 1857 it was recorded *'General Wade made the first visit at Mardale this year.'*

Several people came to the Dun Bull Hotel on more than one occasion. Mr McQueen from Scotland stayed at least three times between 1856 and 1862. Jacob Thompson, the artist, who lived at the Hermitage in Hackthorpe, stayed at least twice between 1856 and 1862. He had been commissioned by Lord Lonsdale to paint various scenes on Haweswater and often stayed in Mardale, which was said to be his favourite place. Another local artist, Thomas Bland, of Reagill stayed in 1859 and drew several sketches of the valley. Many of the visitors complimented the hostess, Mrs Bell, for her lavish hospitality and the quality of the beer which was supplied by Allsops brewery. Guests also praised the food provided. Special mention was made of the ham and eggs which seemed to be the signature dish of the Hotel along with fresh trout from the lake and roast duck and green peas.

Travelling salesman were also regular visitors. In March 1858 a large group stayed including Joseph Tate, Draper of Kendal, G A Hutchinson, Kendal, Fish Hook Manufacturer, Charles Pollitt from the Gazette Office, and Richard Jackson, Tea Dealer and Luke Biggins, Sheffield Butter Dealer. In 1860 Mr Isaac Wilson, Wine Merchant, dined with *'His Majesty, the King of Mardale'* (Mr John Holme) and Sir Thomas Gilpin. Many people left their thoughts in verse. One who signed himself as Tennyson Junior wrote:

'Arrived at the Dun Bull from Shap on 24th at 3pm, stayed all night and left for Patterdale at 9 o'clock

At the site of the Bull
You can eat till youre full
Of fresh trout, eggs, bacon and pancake.
Then if you are dry just Allsops Pale try
And assuredly it will your thirst slake-
But should you want more then there is Oat Cake galore
Besides Tea and Whiskey and Baccy
For Bells Bull Inn I'm sure has a provender store
To please Tourist, Lord, Lady or Lacky.'

The popularity of the Dun Bull grew over the years and was the 'place to be' for the great and the good from far and wide. Many of the visitors arrived at Shap Station, which provided a good starting point from where they would make the five mile walk or be taken by carriage and horses over to Mardale. Not all journeys were easy; an entry in 1859 records:

'Arrived at the Dun Bull after a very enjoyable drive except that the phaeton in which were riding broke into three pieces the front part staying with the horses which bolted leaving us without any locomotion other than we continued on ourselves. We succeeded in getting up a little steam here thanks to our hostess. Jo. Scott and Party. London.'

In 1888 what became known as The Mansion was erected adjacent to the existing building by Mrs Mary Elizabeth Holme. The official name of this house was Greenhead. When she died The Mansion was incorporated into the Dun Bull Hotel providing further accommodation.

With the advent of the motor car in the early twentieth century, the dale became even more accessible. The Dun Bull continued to provide for fisherman, walkers and day visitors who found its old world charm fascinating. The licensee of the Dun Bull was an important cog in the community wheel. At the end of the 19th century Mr and Mrs Baldry, the hoteliers, were part of the group who gave time and money to keep the life of Mardale going. Mr Baldry provided oil for the lamp outside the Church while Mrs Baldry hosted many children's parties at the Dun Bull.

The last landlord of the Dun Bull was a Wiltshire man, Mr Bob Daffurn, who had come north to work as a gardener at Lowther Castle. He left Lowther to become licensee of the Mitre Hotel in Penrith, and then became 'Mine Host' at the Dun Bull in 1906. In the early days of his tenancy he had a stylish horse drawn carriage which he used to transport his guests to and from the stations at Shap and Penrith. Later on a motorised version took its place.

Bob Daffurn's Ford sketched by Dulcie Baily

Bob was a noted breeder of Persian Blue cats. On one occasion a customer had been attracted to a kitten in a basket in the bar and had bought it. A little while later he returned, a little bit upset that he had got a tom cat instead of a female, which he had presumed it to be. He asked if Mr Daffurn really knew anything about cats. After years of experience dealing

Maurice Bell (Bob Daffurn's son-in-law) and kittens

with difficult customers, Bob's charm offensive, combined with one or two whiskeys, placated the gentleman who left quite happy with the kitten.

During his time in Mardale, Bob Daffurn witnessed the coming of change from the early stages. The City of Manchester had centred their urgent need for water on the mountains and valleys of the Lake District and the population of the valleys were aware of the threat to their communities. The opening of the Thirlmere scheme in 1894 may have appeared to remove the threat to Mardale but Manchester Corporation proceeded to buy up the various parcels of land to enable them to proceed with their Haweswater project, and by 1909 a large party from the Manchester Waterworks Committee had visited the valley to view the preliminary work carried out by the early surveyors.

From this time a steady stream of people involved with the building of the dam were accommodated at the Dun Bull, starting with the first surveyors from Manchester who were assessing the suitability of the valley. Although Manchester Corporation took possession of the valley in 1925, it was not until 1928 that it was announced the work of building of the dam would proceed. One very regular visitor to the Dun Bull was Isaac Hinchcliffe, a member of Manchester City Council, who was blamed in some quarters for the decision to flood the valley. In 1933 Bob Daffurn moved to the Greyhound at Shap, leaving his daughter, Mrs Lucy Bell, to wind down the running of the Hotel. When the day finally came to leave, her daughter, Joyce, turned the key for the last time.

Staff at the Dun Bull, 1920s

Hunting Days

Many people find the pastime of hunting for sport and pleasure deeply offensive.

However in the past, especially in deeply rural and impoverished areas, it was necessary for survival. When farm holdings only consisted of a dozen acres or so, the loss of a couple of lambs to the eagle or the fox could be devastating. In the accounts of Shap Church relating to Mardale in 1728 there is a record of payments for the heads of wild animals considered then as pests and vermin. Raven's heads paid at 6d each, wild cats 1s, eagle heads 1s, and foxes 2s 6d to 3s 4d(4) There was no pack of hounds in the valley and the Mardale folk

Hunting party at Mardale, 1922, Joe Bowman seated beside the driver

were obliged to take the control of foxes into their own hands. Canon H D Rawnsley commented in 1906:

'Eagles must have been so plentiful if only a shilling was set on their head. Alas for it, only one eagle of the golden wing has been seen in the lake country in this past year.'(5)

Thomas Yarker, the schoolmaster in Swindale, noted in his diary for the 16th March 1840 that he had been joined by William Graham and Thomas Cowart *'in pursuit of two falcon hawks, one of which they killed. The Hen a very splendid bird weighing about 3lbs and measuring 41inches from one wing tip to the other.'*(6) Although this account refers to the neighbouring valley of Swindale it illustrates the attitudes to wildlife as pests. Possibly these two falcons were attempting to make off with very precious chickens. This need for control developed into regular hunting with hounds which gave the shepherds and farmers a chance for recreation and social contact.

Foxes would have been plentiful in the valley. At the end of the nineteenth century there are records that three hundred foxes were put down in the district without even the help of the Ullswater Foxhounds. The foxhounds visited Mardale regularly and the legendary Mardale Hunt took place in early November, usually combined with sports and the exchange of stray sheep. Canon H D Rawnsley gave a vivid account of his experiences when attending the Mardale Hunt:

'As I was sitting at tea in the Dun Bull the dogs barked and ran furiously into the road. "Dogs is likely comin", said the servant lass, and in another moment Joe Bowman, the well known huntsman of the Ullswater pack and a couple of hounds entered the kitchen."Git oot wilt tha," he cried (Hounds were not allowed in the establishment) and the dogs disappeared like a flash of lightening. Then taking his huntsman's cap off, the stout-built man whose face had been weathered into mahogany with a touch of colour in the stain, bowed to the company and was soon at home with us all. We sat down to tea – haver bread, cheese, tea cakes, jam and apple pasty galore.'

Rawnsley could not stay at the Dun Bull on this occasion and was billeted out at a nearby farm. Later in the evening he returned to the Inn with his host and wrote:

'The breath of the Shepherds meeting had possessed the Dun Bull. Farmers and shepherds who had come over the fells with sheep for the morrow's meeting were sitting on the settles, with their dogs at their feet and with pots of hardly-tasted ale in front of them. Very silent and weary they seemed as well they might be. They had been 'raking' the high fells for the past week in quest of their neighbour's sheep. Presently one whose thoughts were evidently with his dogs out on the moorland said as if he was speaking almost in his sleep, and was addressing nobody in particular, "Ah saw that yan o thine wid t'lamb this morning. Ah tried to git till far side on't byt me dog wasn't 'wiet' eneuf and t'yow bolted and got crag fast, sea ah hed to leave it, but Ah'll have anudder try furst thing i't morning."

A great barking then filled the kitchen and all the dogs rushed out, for the noise of wheels was heard and soon Manchester poured itself into the hostelry. Sturdy young fellows in knickerbockers, in leggings, in shooting jackets and every form of unkempt, rough, untidy dress. Their faces glowed from the frost, their appetites were keen, and we were all of us soon seated round a supper table where 'taty' pot was the principal dish. Then pipes were filled, songs were called for and liquor flowed.'

Rawnsley records that he and his farmer host were admonished on their return to the farm at 10 o'clock, as the wife had threatened to lock them out if they were late back.

'Next morning breakfast was the word. Everyone sat down together, Hunters, Shepherds, Manchester Men, Landlord and Wife.

Joe Bowman

'Poddish, ham and sausage was the fare. Then after Breakfast off out with the hunt.'

This hunt, which Canon H D Rawnsley attended, took place in 1906 when the hunting had become more of a 'sport', with the huntsman and hounds pitting their wits against the wily fox. Many huntsmen, including Joe Bowman, preferred to leave a fox which had gone to earth to live to do battle another day, rather than send terriers down into their bolt holes to kill them.

The hunt ended around noon in time to return to the Dun Bull for another feast. This time the meal was *'Beef boiled and Roast, plum puddings and mince pies.'*

As the accommodation had all been taken up at the Dun Bull by the rowdies from Manchester and he had had to stay elsewhere, Canon H D Rawnsley was not enamoured of some of the visitors who were in attendance at the meet. As he bade adieu and went back towards Shap, he could not help wishing that

'neither Manchester Jovialities or Hurlingham Hospitalities' had been introduced to Mardale. Something of the simplicity of that shepherds meeting in the wilderness had been lost, never to return. But there was also something in the surroundings and in the naturalness of those fine gentlemen-shepherds of the fell which nothing could annul, and the honour of give and take at that shepherd's garth at the Dun Bull was a memory that could not fade, a heritage that no modern invention or invasion could destroy. Gradually all the visitors, shepherds, huntsmen and hounds returned and left the folks of the dale to their peace.

A Shepherds Meet

The Shepherds and their Sheep

Sheep had been kept in the valley since the earliest times, as they were the only domestic animal capable of surviving on the meagre pickings of the high fells. Cattle were kept on the pastures and water meadows lower down but it was the sheep which produced the meat to eat and the wool for clothing. Because the sheep roamed freely over the fells, each farmer gave his animals distinctive marks, mostly with cuts on the ears and dye marks on the wool with each farmer's identification being unique to him. Sheep never strayed very far, for then as now, sheep were heafed, that is they instinctively knew their own territory after generations of breeding and living in the same area.

Isaac Cookson

The sheep were very hardy, they remained on the fells for lambing and were only brought down to the farms for clipping. The shepherds were as hardy as their sheep and walked the fells in all weathers tending their flocks. The iconic image of a Lakeland shepherd, Isaac Cookson, is well known in illustrations of Lakeland life of long ago. Isaac Cookson belonged to the eastern Lake District fells and was well known in Mardale and attended the annual Shepherds' Meet for many years.

For many years the Meet was held on a separate date but gradually the sports and the hunt were added to the agenda for the November festivities and the Hunt and the Meet became a combined event. At the end of the days' hunting, and the feast that followed, the fifty or so shepherds who attended would gather at the pens at the back of the Dun Bull to sort out the stray sheep which had been gathered by them earlier in the week. Long discussions took place as to whom each animal belonged. The keenness of the farmers' eyes in recognising each 'lug and crop mark' without reference to any document was important. They would admit that perhaps the dogs knew their own sheep as well as any shepherd did. *'Dogs ken as weel as ony of us. Ken by t'smell on em, an wad pick em oot leak a man if they war left to theersels.'* (Dogs know as well as any of us. Know by the smell on them and would pick them out like a man if they were left to themselves.)

There would be much chaff about some poor little half-sized creature that no one will own. *"Dusta ken owt about that thing theer, William" "Naay that I divvent: but what! It mud beleng t' thee I'se thinking. Gress upon thy heafs varra poor as we aw knaw at the best of times. Its been a seaun- spaened* yan, I'se thinking."* (*weaned too early). And thus the banter went on until all the sheep were claimed and the shepherds could wend their weary way home. The kindred spirit, which joined these men of the fells with their wry humour and honesty, abounded at these events. Fortunately that spirit has survived and exists among the farming community of the Lake District today.

By the early twentieth century the sports no longer took place, but the Hunt and the Shepherds Meet continued until the last farmers moved away. After the valley was flooded the Meet was held at the St Patricks Well at Bampton and then for a short time at the Haweswater Hotel, but life had changed out of all recognition even for the farming community and the event became a mere shadow of its former days.

The last hunt

John Graham recalls:

'One of the valley characters was the local postman, Ronnie Scott. He would start his day's journey from Bampton Post Office delivering mail up to, and including, Mardale, arriving at the Dun Bull about 11.15am. A letter box in the wall opposite the lane to Goosemire had to be emptied at 2pm so Ronnie had approximately three hours to spend at the 'Dunny'. He was not a loafer and could turn his hands to many odd jobs, for instance he would help with the hay at hay time or with sheep on clipping or dipping days or mow the lawn or any other task that was in need of a helping hand. In return he had a free lunch plus the odd pint or two. There were days now and then when no jobs needed doing, so Ronnie would perhaps imbibe an extra pint or so. On one such occasion Ronnie set off on his return journey, emptying the aforesaid letterbox on his way, but further on and being slightly 'tipsy' failed to negotiate a corner and landed in a heap with his bike in the hedge. He was trying to extricate himself from his bike and regain his feet when a local farmer came around the corner, and seeing Ronnie's predicament, went to his aid. On helping him to his feet and straightening his cap and tie, he enquired what had happened. The good Samaritan got a very sharp and brusque reply "Well, that damned corner wasn't there yesterday."

Ronnie Scott, Joyce, Maurice Bell and huntsmen

The Dun Bull

Chapter 7

The Schools

'Tis education forms the common mind,
Just as a twig is bent, the tree's inclined.'

Alexander Pope – Epistles to Several Persons 'To Lord Cobham' (1734)

The earliest mention of education in Mardale is the founding of a grammar school at Measand in 1711 by Richard Wright and Richard Law, the third of the free grammar schools founded in the parish of Bampton. It is likely that anyone wishing to receive an education before this would have attended the Free Grammar School at Bampton which had been founded by Thomas Sutton in 1623. Another school, Rough Hill, to the west of Bampton was endowed by Edmund Noble in 1663. Richard Law gave the site on which the old school was constructed, and the school master was entitled to certain 'whittlegate' in Measand. This was the privilege of clergy and schoolmasters to dine at each house in the parish in turn (i.e. using his 'whittle' or knife). In some instances the 'guests' stayed a week at each farm. This custom prevailed into the nineteenth century.

Carlisle says of Measand:(1)

"In 1723 Richard Law of Cawdale gave a garth in which the school stands. The Westminster grammars are chiefly used. The present master is Mr Joseph Wharton whose salary and emoluments are about £42 per annum.'

A copy of the original indenture reads:

"This indenture made the twentieth day of October in the tenth yeare of the reign of our Sov'aine Lady Anne by the grace of God Queen of great Brittaine of ffrance and Ireland Defendr if the ffaith &c. and in the yeare of our Lord God , one thousand seaven hundred

and eleaven, Between Richard Wright Snr of Meason in the Parish of Bampton in the County of Wesm"land Yeoman of the one part, and John Holme of Riggendale and Richard Holme of Meason and Thomas Holme of Meason all in the Parish of Bampton aforesaid Yeomn of the other part. Wittnesseth that the said Richard Wright for and in considerac'on of the great love and affection which he hath and beareth for and towards the Inhabitants of adjacent Townships and Villages and for promoting and advancing of vertue and piety by Learning and good discipline and to that end erecting and Building a School-house in Meason aforesaid and afterwards for repairing of the same and for the maintaining of a fitt and well qualified person as may teach English and Grammar Schoole within the same."

The school was endowed by the Holmes with properties at Nether Scales and Scale Park in Orton - called Overton in the indenture.

The document continues:

"The trustees of the sd school shall doe out the rent issues and profitts of the said Granted premisies uphold and keep in good and sufficient repair a School-house built or intended to be built at Meason aforesaid by the said Richard Wright his executrs Admrs or Asignes and also shall maintain and keep a fitt and well qualified person to teach English and Latin tongue and any other good literature as is usually taught at other Grammar Schools within the same. The whole rents and profits of the said Granted premises being intended for the maintenance of the School Master for ever, and for repairing the School-house to be built at Meason as aforesiad, and also Twelve shillings to be yearly deducted and paid out of the said Rents and profitts towards the buying of Books for so many Poor Schollars as shall learne or be taught at the school."

The trustees were to be chosen from people or inhabitants living within the limits or district of Measand, Little Water, Drybarrows, Whelter, Flakehow and Riggindale, all within the parish of Bampton.

The school was free for both sexes - quite a privilege at a time when female education was a rarity. The hours of attendance were from six in the morning to six at night except for an hour from eight to nine for breakfast and from twelve to two for dinner. The education provided a good grounding in the classics, written English and Latin and other good literature – it is said that the farm boys spoke Latin to their horses. The school was a very small building, with little or no accommodation, so pupils were boarded out at local farms.

Towards the end of the nineteenth century the old school

Measand Grammar School

building became a cottage, but has the distinction of being the only complete building to have been rescued from the flooding; it was dismantled and re-erected at Walmgate Head.

Richard Law inherited the estate of his uncle Richard Wright and had his name inscribed on the tablet above the door below that of the founder, adding the date 1713. They are listed respectively as founder and benefactor. Richard Law was one of the family of Edmund Law, Bishop of Carlisle who had thirteen children, three of his sons John, Edward and George created something of a record at Cambridge by becoming one after the other classical medallists in combination with the second and third wranglerships – this record is believed never to have been equalled. John Law became Bishop of Clonfert in Ireland, Edward became Chief Justice to the King's Bench and later Lord Ellenborough, George became Bishop of Bath and Wells.

Most masters of Measand were also the incumbent of Mardale. Although many names will also appear in the list of vicars of Mardale in Chapter 5, these men were often appointed as master first, and then at a later date were appointed as curate. Early headmasters were nominated jointly by the vicars of Shap and Bampton. A sequence of worthy men are recorded as masters beginning with Michael Sommers who was *'Licentia concesa est Michaeli Somers Diacono ad per agendum officium Curati et ad (educandos) pueros in Capella de Mardale.'* He was appointed as curate of Mardale on 24th May 1703 and became curate of Shap in 1708. From the Latin extract it would seem that he was to provide some education for children in the chapel prior to the foundation of the school.

William Langhorn is believed to have been appointed in 1708 as master of Measand, and was the father of William Langhorn, vicar of Shap. Other masters were:

1722-25 Jonathan Tinclair, master of Measand, and founder of Tinclair's Library at Bampton Vicarage (now housed in Bampton church hall)

1725-26 William Robinson MA, reader and master of Measand

1726-31 Thomas Baxter was appointed *'to read prayers and teach school'* in Mardale Chapel. He was ordained Deacon in June 1728

1731-34 Richard Holme, Deacon appointed to preach the Word of God in the chapel or elsewhere in the Diocese of Carlisle.

1734-39 William Collinson, Master of Measand

1731 John Watson, licensed as Master of Measand and was appointed curate of Mardale in 1739. He became the minister of Shap in 1741.

1741-49 Bartholomew Hayes, Reader and Master of

Measand, was nominated by the vicar of Bampton, the curate of Shap, and principal residents, and was licensed as curate in September 1742.

1749-99 Richard Hebson was Master for fifty years. He was nominated by the vicars of Shap and Bampton and by the principal inhabitants. A stone tablet on the porch of Mardale church, and now at Shap, reads:

To the Memory
Of the Revd Ri: Hebson upwards of 50 years The truly Christian Pastor of this Chapelry. And the able and most diligent Master of Measand School for a still longer period.
He died Septr. 25th 1799 Aged 75
Reader
This stone pretends not to be the record of his virtues; they built not their hopes on such perishable materials; but only a small token of grateful attention from one who profited by his instructions and reveres the example he set of unaffected conscientious Integrity.

The joint nomination of Hayes and Hebson is worthy of note and came about through four causes: the carving of the chapelry out of the two parishes; the non-existence of a 'real vicar' at Shap; the frequent attachment of the school at Measand, which is in Bampton parish, to the readership; and the privilege accorded to the vicar of Bampton of ministering in the chapel from time to time.

On 22nd October 1800 John Bowstead, or 'Auld Boosty' as he was called, became master of Measand and stayed until 1843. When he was master of Bampton, the school gained a considerable reputation as a theological college which, like St. Bees, turned out hundreds of local priests such as Rowlandson and Holme of Shap, and Walker and Sewell of Swindale. A painting of Bowstead can be seen in Bampton Church Hall, in which he is pictured wearing a rather angular hat and with a hooked nose. His pupils presented him with a snuff box. He had a reputation, not only as a scholar, but as a raconteur in local dialect which he used when conversing with farmers and friends.

In her book Mary Noble[2] lists Mr Greenhow as a master, but does not indicate when. Parson & White's Gazeteer published in 1829[3] tells us that *'The free school here was founded in 1713 by Richard Wright and Richard Lacy, who endowed it with an estate, now worth upwards of £40. a year: the Rev. John Greenhow is the present master.'*

The last master was Jonathan Rigg who came to Measand and is recorded in the 1841 census, he was a widower with a daughter, and employed a housekeeper. He died in 1877, leaving his estate to his daughter.

The Education Act was passed in 1870, and was intended to provide education on an unprecedented scale. School boards were introduced and given the power to create new schools and pay the fees of the poorest children. It was a condition of these Board Schools that all children should attend school between the ages of five and thirteen years. By 1880 many new schools had been set up by the boards, which meant that the Education Act of 1880 could make school attendance compulsory for all children up to the age of ten.

'The first duty of the State is to see that every child born therein shall be well housed, clothed, fed and educated, till it attain the years of discretion.'

John Ruskin - Time and Tide (1867) - Letter 13.

The Mardale School, situated at Whelter, was built in 1883. It was officially known as Measand Mardale School, because some of the endowments granted to Measand Grammar School were transferred to the new school. The first master was Ebenezer Wilks. Miss Jane Forster was appointed as school mistress at Mardale in 1891 at the age of 23 years. She was born at Laithes near Penrith and had applied for a teaching position in Westmorland. The Mardale position was the only one with a house, which enabled her to bring her parents from Thursby to live with her in the school house.

Miss Forster remained in the dale for the rest of her working life and kept a wonderful record in her precise copperplate hand, detailing the lessons and achievements of her pupils.[4] A governors' report in 1895 states they were pleased with Miss

Mardale School

Forster's work finding the surroundings *'cheerful'*. Although Miss Forster was the only teacher, her records give details of three classes, although these could simply have referred to age groups or abilities. The subjects taught were: Reading, Writing, Arithmetic, Mental Arithmetic, Recitation, Needle-work, Drawing, English, Object lessons, Varied occupation, Singing and Drill.

The books used for teaching reading, included Great Authors, with History, Geographical, Royal and Science readers, and Anderson's Fairy Tales. Writing consisted mainly of exercises and copy book work. Arithmetic lessons included multiplication and division of vulgar fractions and decimals, addition and subtraction to tens of thousands, long division and multiplication with multipliers to 99, the pupils also practiced addition of money. Mental arithmetic included questions about the rules of arithmetic and tables, and it would appear from Miss Forster's comments that some of the children in Class Two found the problems difficult to understand and work requiring intelligent thought was not done readily.

Recitation involved reading poetry and explaining the meaning of the text, there are notes to say that expression had improved. In needle-work classes (presumably for the girls only) new stitches were taught and work from home was brought to school, garments were also made. Drawing consisted of making various freehand and ruled copies and also geometry. English involved learning the different parts of the language such as verbs, adjectives, nouns, pronouns, parsing and analysis, breaking down passages into the various components, punctuation and definition, there also seemed to have been a lot of work on adjectives and adverbs.

Object lessons covered a wonderfully wide range of topics such as how plants feed, lead pencils, friction, milk, volcanoes, glow-worms, the cuckoo and swallow, leaves, butter and churning, bee-keeping, and most topically, a farm and the seasonal jobs such as sheep washing and shearing, and haymaking. Varied occupation seems to have mainly consisted of crayon work and making rag mats but every child looked forward to these lessons. Singing included tonic sol-fa exercises and set songs, whilst drill was done to approved exercises.

In February 1896 the Day School prize books were presented for regular attendance and good conduct. Each child received a book varying in value according to the attendance, but all seem to have done very well in that respect. Miss Forster presented the books, and the Vicar gave a magic lantern display. The school inspector wrote: *'This school is conducted in a quiet, steady and unassuming though thoroughly efficient manner, and the scholars are progressing satisfactorily."*

The school room was opened each Friday evening between 6 and 9pm for the boys and young men to enjoy reading and games, with elementary science lessons on magnetism, electricity and wood carving.

In May 1897 Miss Forster noted *'There is only one boy in Standard two and one in Standard one, so they have worked together at all the subjects except Arithmetic. They have only been on the Register about 10 weeks and the Standard one boy has attended very badly, being subject to chronic bronchitis."* There is also a note that *"Dorothy Greenhow is falling away with her attainments, she is not able to attend school regularly during the winter months as her home is at some distance, and she has delicate health.'* (The family lived at Naddle.)

The roll of pupils that year listed: Annie Edmondson, John Forster, Arthur Terry, Brunskill Kitching, Hugh Kitching, Thomas Mounsey, Arthur Kitching, Thomas Edmondson, John Mounsey, Dorothy Greenhow, Hannah Edmondson, William H. Oliver, Oswald Baldry, Edwin Oliver and Clifford Evans.

The Edmondsons lived at Flakehow, the Kitchings at Measand, the Mounseys at Whelter, Arthur Terry was the Vicar's son, and Oswald Baldry was the son of the landlord at the Dun Bull, John Forster was Miss Forster's nephew who lived at the school house; the homes of the Oliver and Evans boys are unknown. In 1897 Miss Forster made some general remarks for all the classes:

'The work during the 4th Quarter has been chiefly recapitulation of previous works and doing exam tests on the various subject. The Science and Art Department have awarded the 'Excellent' mark for Drawing, and the Government Report is as follows: – 'Writing and Arithmetic have been well taught, but the instruction in Reading and Recitation has been less successful than in previous years and improvement in these subjects will be looked for as a condition of continued recommendation of the higher principal grant. The full rate for English is also awarded with much hesitation. Needlework is good. The order and tone of the school continue quite satisfactory.'

Principal Grant for 14 children @	*14/0 each*
Discipline and Organisation	*1/6*
Singing	*1/0*
English	*2/0*
Total	*18/6*
Sewing 5 @ 2/0 =	*10/0*
Grant on Average	*£12 19s 0d*
Grant on sewing	*10s 0d*
	Total £13 9s 0d"

In 1898, the Government report stated: *'The tone and order of this small school is very good. The instruction is carefully given, and it is creditably successful. Since the last inspection an improvement has been effected in the style of reading also in English, which no doubt will be carried further. Drawing mark – Excellent.'*

The school received many distinguished visitors, including Sir Joseph Savoury, the Member of Parliament for Appleby, and Lady Savoury, with Captain Markham and Mrs Markham from Morland.

In 1897 the school was found to have a problem of damp on the west wall, and in 1898 the west end of the schoolroom was panelled in an effort to cure the problem, this work being carried out by Wilson Ewbank of Bampton. There was a smoke problem in the school house kitchen, and the Vicar and Mr Christopher Wilson were appointed as a committee of two to see this work carried out. This was expected to be costly so an appeal was issued to the farmers of the district who had children attending the school to agree to cart any material free of charge. A later entry says that *'the large outlay on the School buildings seems at least so far as we can judge to be quite justified.'* They did not expect any further problems with damp or smoke, the walls had been painted and proved a distinct improvement. A new case had been provided for the harmonium which would also serve as a cutting-out table, a set of plant pots had been provided for the windows, and new pictures had been hung on the walls.

In 1900 the Government report on the school was satisfactory, the highest grant being earned. The following shows the balance sheet for the year:

Receipts	**Expenses**
Grants from Department	£41 13s 6d
Salaries	£71 13s 6d
Fee Grant	£8 7s 6d
Books and Stationery	£1 19s 7d
Taken from Endowment	£32 17s 11d
Apparatus	10s 0d
Fuel and cleaning	£3 14s 4d
Repairs to Building	£4 6s 6d
Rates	£5 0s 6d
Organising Secretary	10s 0d
Total	£82 18s 11d

Miss Forster and pupils on the last day of school, 1932

During the month of June the school was closed due to an epidemic of whooping cough. In the census of 1901, the occupants of the school house include a 10 year old girl, Elizabeth Jane Farrar, who was described as the Forster's grand daughter.

By 1901 the number of children had decreased, so Miss Forster was paid a fixed salary of £70 per annum, instead of the salary being dependent on a government grant. The Inspector's report was again favourable with the highest grant being earned, there was a recommendation that the school roof be repaired. This was done using Westmorland slates at the cost of £60, met from ordinary receipts with the carting being done free. The accounts showed a total of £78.18s 10d. The Inspector's report was countersigned by the Bishop as encouraging, the Inspector wrote that:

'This small school has received careful and conscientious instruction, and the children had a bright and pleasing manner. They were attentive and interested, and a few showed readiness and intelligence. The facts of the Bible were generally known and the examination of the Prayer Book and Catechisms were satisfactory. The repetition was accurate, but said too rapidly and without expression. A very nice tone prevails in the school.'

In 1902 two pupils received medals for good attendance. The balance sheet showed £88.10s 8½d. The Diocesan Inspector visited and wrote:

'The school has declined in numbers owing to the removal of some families from the parish. The teacher has again discharged this department of her duties with great care and sympathy. The children possessed a good and ready knowledge of their work, and took pleasure in giving answers. The singing was devout and sweet, the hymns having been carefully chosen. The memory work was correctly given.'
The report was initialled by the Bishop as most satisfactory.

In that same year, the school farm at Low Scales, Orton (granted to Measand School) was sold at auction for £1,400, the income having steadily declined for some years previously. The money was to be invested in securities approved by the Charity Commissioners, and it was hoped that the interest would equal or exceed the rent received. The investment was placed in three per-cent perpetual debenture stock of the London and North Western railway Company. In 1903 the Government Inspector reported on Measand Mardale School:

'This remote little school is well managed by Miss Forster. Geography, a comparatively new subject, is not equal to other work. The Managers have greatly improved the condition of the premises.'
The balance sheet showed £149 1s 11d. Two medals for perfect attendance were awarded to Elizabeth J Farrar and Joseph

Mounsey, who had won them in 1902. A new Board of Managers were elected to manage the three schools of Bampton, Mardale and Roughill, they were named as Miss Noble of Beckfoot, Mr W. Little of Penrith, who were foundation managers, the Vicars of Bampton and Mardale, Mr A Wright appointed by the County Council, Mr John Dargue appointed by Bampton Parish Council and Mr M Sarginson as clerk to the governors. The Diocesan Inspector called again and made a very searching examination lasting one and a half hours; he found the school to be well maintained and very satisfactory. In 1904 His Majesty's Inspector reported:

'Although the school is remote, and there are only a few children on the books, the work proceeds quietly and pleasantly, and the progress made is quite satisfactory.'

The Diocesan Inspector found the religious instruction to have received the best attention of the teacher. At the recommendation of the Inspector a scripture prize, of a valuable book, was awarded to Elizabeth Farrar, and the medals for perfect attendance were presented to Elizabeth Farrar and Joseph Mounsey (both for the third year running) and Agnes Hudson, who also received a medal the following year, with her brother Hugh.

In 1906 when the Diocesan Inspector visited, no less than four pupils had perfect attendance and received medals – Elizabeth Farrar, Agnes Hudson, Hannah Watson, Hugh Hudson, and three of them – Hannah Watson, Agnes Hudson and Hugh Hudson – received books from the Richard Rawes Charity, Shap, for good attendance and conduct. The Vicar's prize for efficiency at the examination was awarded to Ethel Burn and Agnes Hudson. A framed engraving was awarded to Mardale School by Westmorland County Council Education Committee for the high percentage of attendances during the previous year. Miss Forster's father John Forster, a retired farmer, died in 1907 aged 85, and her mother, Jane, died in 1917 aged 82; they were interred in Thursby church yard.

In 1918 there were twelve pupils but by 1927 only seven remained. Tommy Edmondson recalled:

'Kitchings fra Measand, he was boatman for ' Earl o' Lonsdale a''

th' hed sixteen in family, ther was allus six er sebben et school; the' hed a hard bringin' up, the' wad walk fra Measand te school, a mile an a half; on stormy days the' war wet throo afore the' got te Mardle school, the hed a hard life. Ther' was Howarths at Riggindale farm, they hed a couple o' lads thet went te school, and the' kept a servant lass. And once er twice a week she was bring these two lads the'r dinner te school, a hot potato pie mebbe. Noo when th'ed hed wat the wanted, the wad scoop up wat was left an thow it up te t' ceilin' and ye sud ha seen them la'al nippers dive in te eat t' scraps – aye the hed a hard life.'

Children from farming families were in the habit of taking time off school at busy times such as clipping, hay making and harvest to help at home. They were also liable to go off to follow the hunt, although this was not allowed, and they had to suffer the consequences.

The school closed in 1932, and a photograph shows Miss Forster with her last few pupils. A mantel clock presented to her on her retirement is still in existence, the plaque on it reads *'For services rendered Mardale 1891-1932 From old scholars and friends.'*

Miss Forster remained in the school house until the very end, when she moved to Rayside to live with her niece and her husband, Mr and Mrs Mark Lowis. As well as her detailed school records Miss Forster had made a scrapbook of cuttings from Ruridecanal Magazines[5] mentioning events in Mardale, alongside other cuttings from local newspapers. These have proved invaluable to researchers.

The school doubled as a community hall, and was the venue of clubs for girls and boys. There was a reading room and frequent lectures, concerts and lantern shows took place. These lantern shows were so popular that the lantern was converted from a lamp to gas to provide better light, a brighter picture and less danger.

A parish library was opened in 1896 and was open every Sunday. The Yorkshire Institute and Village Library offered a loan of a 100 books to be kept for a year then exchanged for a further supply. There was a small annual subscription, but as they were able to select their own books from the 32,000 volumes it was felt to be worth every penny. The following year there was an appeal for the return of books so that they could be returned to Leeds, and a further supply would be sent for the winter months. In 1899 it is recorded that the new supply of books numbered 300 volumes, and that the library was now known as the Parish Lending Library.

The boy's club had classes in woodcarving and science and an appeal was made for old publications such as the Illustrated London News. The items made at the clubs were sold to defray the expense of tools and materials. The Girls Club enjoyed games, magazines, picture books, and a series of short lectures on domestic economy given by Miss Forster, with sewing supervised by Mrs Terry and Mrs Hudson. The Vicar gave elementary lessons in music. The Girls Club came under the umbrella of the Girls Friendly Society which was founded in 1875 in England by Mary Elizabeth Townsend. It was the first organisation for women in the Church of England and provided a place where unmarried girls could experience friendship and recreation in a fellowship of Christian love and service. This new organisation later adopted the title of the Girl's Friendly Society.

A branch of the Band of Hope, a temperance movement, was formed and run by Miss Forster, in 1902 the Vicar gave a lecture entitled 'Alcohol: what it is and what it can do'.

Social evenings and dances were held, with a party at Christmas. One popular event was the annual tea and concert. In 1897 this was attended by 80 people, food being contributed by several people, with many more taking part in the concert. The proceeds were used for parish needs such as forms (benches) for the school, and to

MARDALE CONCERT,

PROGRAMME

Selection,	Shoulder arms March,	Military Band
Song,	Merry, little, fat, gray man,	Rev. W. Terry
Song,	Mary of Argyle,	Miss M. Dufton
Song,	Joe Powman, Patterdale huntsman,	Mr. R. Winster
Song,	Bailiff's daughter of Islington,	Miss A. Hudson
Song,	A Soldier and a Man,	Mr. Scott
Stump speech,	The milk in the cocoa nut,	Mr M'Ginn
Piccolo solo,	The deep blue sea,	Mr. Eli Hudson
Duet,	Larboard Watch,	Mr. Winster and the Vicar
Song,	The Banks of Allan Water,	Miss Wharton
Song,	Money,	Mr. Hindson
Song,	Cherry ripe,	Miss Ethel Burn
Humorous Song,	Flat footed Jean,	Mr. Burn
Quartette,	The Sailors' Chorus,	Quartette Party

HUMOROUS SKETCH, ENTITLED—

'Our New Pawn Shop'

CHARACTERS

Miss H. Edmondson,—Pawnbroker, Miss A. Edmondson—a Widow in deep trouble, Maggie Edmondson,—a poor little girl, Mr J. Forster,—a fast young Swell, Mr J. Hindson,—Peg-Leg Mr T, Thompson,—a drunkard. hard up, Mr Wm. Thompson, Blackman, hard up too. Master Hudson,—The Shop boy. Mr G. Salkeld,—The Policeman.

Selection,	The Gladiator's farewell,	Military Band
Song,	Hard times come again no more,	Rev, W. Terry
Song,	Chiming Bells of long ago,	Miss A. Hudson
Song,	The Farmer's boy.	Mr. R. Winster
Song,	The Hen Convention,	Fred Burn
Song,	Good old Jeff,	Miss M. Dufton
Comic song,	The Singing master,	Mr Mc'Ginn
Banjo solo,	Home, sweet home,	Mr Oakley
Song,	Three makes jolly fine company,	Mr. Scott
Song,	The Wishing gate,	Miss Wharton
Reading,	A Westmorland crack,	Mr. J. Forster
Song,	The Mardale hunt,	Mr. Hindson
Comic song,	Fishing,	Mr Mc' Ginn
Song,	I love the merry merry sunshine,	Miss Ethel Burn
Humorous Song,	The Registrar,	Mr. Burn

GOD SAVE THE KING.

The Audience will sing the Choruses. Chorus papers provided.

pay the subscription for the Library.

Lectures were given on topics of interest in the valley, especially on farming here and abroad. An illustrated lecture on Farms and Farming in Canada was given in school. Mr W. T. Lawrence, Principal of the Cumberland and Westmorland Farm School at Newton Rigg, Penrith gave an illustrated lecture on 'Successful Poultry Keeping.' The Vicar gave an illustrated lecture on Farming in Queensland with a collection of slides loaned by the Government of that colony. In 1897 Mr Christopher Wilson, a Barrister of Walmgate Head, Bampton presented to the parish a copy of the original deed constituting Measand Grammar School. This was an interesting document which was placed in the church chest for safekeeping.

In 1898 the Ruridecanal Magazine recorded the postal alterations.

'In addition to the advantage of an earlier delivery and later collection of letters which we have now enjoyed for some months, the Postmaster General has acceded to the petition sent from Measand and Mardale some time ago, and given permission for the postman to carry heavier parcels and take passengers.'

In addition to this, arrangements were made to commence a penny bank in Mardale, in connection with the Post Office Savings Bank. It was to be open each Monday at the school from 12 to 12.30, and on Monday evenings at the Vicarage from 7 to 7.30 commencing on Monday 6th March. Sums of money from 1d upwards could be invested and interest at the rate of 2¼ % on each complete pound was paid by the Government. Withdrawals could be made at any time by giving a week's notice and bank books were supplied free. A year later it was recorded that over £22 had been deposited, of that about £7 was credited to the children; everyone was advised to save, *'for it would most certainly be useful one day.'*

In the November the Men's Reading Room was opened. It was furnished with a bagatelle board, chess, draughts, together with daily, weekly and monthly issues of papers and magazines. Smoking was allowed in the effort to make the room as attractive as possible to the men. A committee was formed to run this club. In March 1899 the season closed with a social evening, the highlight being a bagatelle match between Measand and Mardale, with Measand the winner. This was followed by a knife and fork supper, then games and music. The Boys and Girls clubs closed for the summer but held two gatherings for tea and games. The Annual Tea and Concert, followed by a dance, was attended by 40 couples.

In 1903 Mardale had the pleasure of a visit from a parishioner of 20 years ago, Mr W T Martindale, formerly of Flakehow but now a prosperous farmer near Victoria, Vancouver Island, British Columbia. His advice to steady, hardworking young men, who had no apparent prospects in England, was summed up in a few words and amounted to this: *'Come out to Canada but come soon.'*

In 1905 a Rifle Club was formed. *'The Club is taking shape very rapidly. Dr Ashby, the president, has very generously provided a valuable rifle and 600 rounds of practice ammunition. A second rifle of less power has also been placed at the service of the members, and a range and make-shift target have also been provided. Captain Parkin, Lowther and Lieut. H Little, Hutton Hall, Penrith have written warmly commending the work, and accepting the office of Vice Presidents. The Vicar will act as secretary pro. tem. Nine members have joined at the time of writing, and we want at least twenty. We can commence practice any time.'*

In 1907, the club was affiliated to the Society of Miniature Rifle Clubs which meant that members did not need to hold a gun licence. A rifle that had seen service during the Boer War was presented by Lt. Little and a thousand rounds of ammunition were donated by Mr A Pearson.

Despite living in a remote valley community, Mardallians enjoyed a lively social life, and were familiar with current news events. They were aware of other parts of the globe through the popular lantern shows and lectures which featured such places as Australia, Canada, Africa, Switzerland, Japan, Egypt, the Holy Land, India and Norway.

Chapter 8

Wills and Inventories of some Mardale Families

The earliest will recorded from Mardale at the county archives is that of Edward Jackson dated 1564. All early wills began in a similar way, often made when the person was 'sick in Body but in perfitt memory.' The first and most important consideration was to make sure that the soul was taken care of, a priority in late medieval times, so the opening sentence began by 'commending my soul to almyghtye god' followed by instructions for burial 'my body to be sepulted in the pariche churche yarde at Shappe with all dewtes of Ryght there to belonging.'

The contents of the 16th century wills illustrate the simplicity and, by today's standards, the impoverished nature of the possessions of the deceased. Various amounts of wool were bequeathed. Wool was a valuable commodity when most clothes were made from homespun, a cloth made from wool woven at home and made into garments either by travelling tailors or the people themselves. The men folk were often as efficient at making clothes as the women.

Edward Jackson was one of the tenants at Naddle and made his will in 1565. His will follows the customary pattern and although his possessions were meagre the inventory which follows is quite detailed:

Will of Edward Jackson

In the name of god Amen the 17th day of december 1565 I Edward Jackson seke in bodye but of perfitt memorye doe make this my Last Will and testament in maner and furme folowinge first I commend my soule to almyghty god, my Bodye to be sepulted in the parish churche yard at shappe with all duetes of Ryght therto belonginge: Item I geve unto Roger my son a gared cowe 2 hogges and crone olde sheppe Item I geve unto margat my daughter one blake cowe a bronne backed Whye two hogges and one ould sheppe with a great Brasse pott. Item I geve unto wyllm my son a blacke Whye The rest of all my other goods my detts legases and funerals discharged and payed I geve unto elles my Wife and my 7 childrynge mychell Anthony Wylliam John Roger mabell and margat whome I make my hole executores and I order Robert Jackson henrye chappelhowe HenreJackson and Wylliam Jackson my supervisors Wyttenesses Alexander Jackson gylbert mesnnt John Lowes and Jeffery Whinfell [curate ibis?]

A list of Edward Jackson's debts is also given:

A debitorye out of the said goods

Item Alexander burges for a stone of Wolle	*7s*
Item to John Jackeson for Wolle	*7s*
Item to John for a pott of oille	*4d*
Item to the Wyfe of myles tomson for Weving one Web	*4d*
	Summa totalis 9s 8d

The will of Richard Holme dated 16th July 1604 confirms the existence of the Chapel in Mardale (*'I gyve to the Chapell of mardall two shillings'*) and also the fact that burial took place at the Parish Church of Shap (*'my bodie to be buryid in my parishe churche of Shape painge the dutes there unto belonginge '*) Three William Holmes were dwelling in the valley at this time, one at Chapel Hill, one at Whelter and a third, the son of Richard, whose dwelling place is not recorded.

Will of Richard Holme 1604

In the name of God Amene on the 15th Day of marche anno domini 1603, I Rychard Hollme sicke in bodie yette in parfit and good remembranc maiks this my last Will and testament in manner & forme following; firste I bequethe my soule unto Almyghte God my maikar and to Jeysus Christe my Redeemare, and my bodie to be buryid in my parishe churche of Shape painge the dutes there unto belonginge I give unto my eldeste sonne Thomas fortie of my beste gymmar shepe ewes or gymmars whear he lykes beste and for the shepe he calles hys owne he shall have nonne of theme exepte he laik of

theme to maike up his fortie Also I gyve unto my sonne Thomas sixe weathers and a tope haye and all my chests and arks one chest exeptit to my doughtar Issabell and all my husbandre geare and my great Calldrann Also I gyve unto my sonne Wylliam tenne of my beste gymar hogs and tenne ewes or gymmars wheare my sonne Thomas will taik theme for hyme and a ewe and a hoge he calls his own and my beste [topper?] Also I gyve unto my thre doughtars thre of my best whyes syxe puthere plattars that I bought my selfe equallye to devide amongst theme my beste brasse potte to my Doughtar Issabell and to my Doughtar Elizabethe two weathers that she calls her owne: Also I gyve to the Chapell of mardall two shillings and to the elmfowld bridge twelve pence Also I maike my hole executors of almy goods payable my wyfe Elizabethe my sonne Wylliam and my thre Doughtars that is Elizabeth Isabell and Jenneyt my dets And leggasses And all expenses discharged Also I maike suparvissars of this my last will and testament Christofer Cowparthwayt of kentmere william holme of chapell hill william holme of wheltar and willm holme of mardell.
Proved 16th July 1604

Although John Airey made his will in 1601 he was to live for another nine years. The contents illustrate the complexities of debts to various people, whether for rent of land, purchases or legacies owing to family members.

Will of John Airey 1611

In the name of god Amen, the 14th day of may in the yeare of our Lord god 1601 I John Aray of meason in the parishe of Bampton sicke in bodye but whole and perfect in Rememberannce thankes be unto god do make this my last will and Testament in maner and forme followinge fyrst I gyve and bequeathe my Soule into the handes of Almeightye god my Savioure and Redemer trustinge onelye to be saved by Jesus Christ his deathe and my bodye to be buryed in my parishe churche yerd, besyde my childrenn. Item I gyve and bequeathe to my sonne george Aray all my Land and tenantright in meason, and my Wyfe to be his gardener till he come to one and twentye yeares of age. Item I gyve to my doughter margaret a gymer hogg, and to my doughter Ellen Aray one gymmer hogge. I Am indebted unto my mother at whitsuntyde next a 11s. I do owe unto my sister doughter Agnes Thomson fyve pounds, otes. I do owe to my sister maryan Aray 42s-8d, to be paid betwane mychalmas and martynmas, Item gyv to my sister Elizabethe Aray, of her child portion, 46s-8d and 9s concerninge hyr legasye to be paid betwene Saint Andrews day and Christemas Item I am indebted unto Henrye dennesson dwellinge with Thomas hudson for sex yowes to be paid at all Saincts day 24s, I do owe unto Rycharde wilkinson of Eysebarrow 15s 6d and for a wedg and a gavelocke 5s wherof 2s is paid. Item I do owe unto mathew wilkinson of knipe 11d, I do owe for the churche money 20s, and to henrye baxter wyfe 40s, to be paid at mychalmas, I do owe unto Elizabeth Jackson for sex busshells of corne and a halfe, 21s 8d to be paid at lammas day next. I do owe unto marye denny 12s to be paid at our Ladye day next. I do owe unto Isabell lowes of swindale 13s 4d to be paid at our Ladye day next. Item I do owe unto Richard fearann £5 for a bill to be paid at fyve candelmas days whereof one is past and the other to come Item I am indebted to Roland denny 10s and to henry denny 4s Item I do owe unto heughe gybson of knype £3 6s 8d to be paid at candelmas day next. I do owe unto Leonard machell 26s 8d to be paid at lamas day next. I do owe unto henrye denneson 32s to be paid at lamas Day come a twelmonth I do owe unto John hutblacke 17s to be paid at lamasday next Item I ame indebted unto John Robinson of wynder 16s, to be paid at lamas day next. Item I gyve unto my sonne George Aray all my wargeare and my husbanrye geare and a great chyst in the netherend of the house Item I gyve unto my wyfe one chiste Called the brodeinge for her lyfe All the Rest of my goods moveable and unmoveable I gyve to my daughters Ellen Aray and margaret Aray whom I make executors of this my last will my debtes and funerall expenses paid and dischared Witnesses hereof henrye hodgson John Jackson Thomas hudson Rych Aray Cuthbert herrison"

Inventory of John Airey 1611

The trew Inventory of the goods moveable and unmoveable of John Aray of meason prysed by 4 men Roger Jackeson Jaimes bowman John hotblacke henrye hodgson 29th may 1610

Item his apparell	*28s*
Item for Iron geare and other implements	*12s*
Item Wargeare	*7s*
Item plowgeare	*5s*
Item puder vessels with other implements	*12s*
Item wargeare	*7s*
Item plowgeare	*5s*
Item puder vessels with potts and pannes	*22s*
Item beddinge	*3s 4d*
Item two chests and a arke	*10s*
Item wood vessels with tubbes and gylefatts	*10s*
Item crokes and other Iron Implements	*7s 4d*
Item bourdes and sleddes with other implements	*20d*
Item [..] malt and [..] seckes & bigg	*25s*
Item sede and [. . .]	*32s*
Item [..] kine	*£4 13s 4d*
Item 58 sheepe	*£14 10s*
Item one horse skyn	*20d*
Item one Amerye	*10s*
Suma	*£31 10s*

Debts of John Airy 1611

John Aray his debtes as followes

To margaret Aray	*11s*
To Agnes Thomson	*£5*
To maryan Aray	*46s 8d*
To Elizabethe Aray	*46s 8d*
and for her legasye	*9s*
To henrye denneson	*24s*
To Rychrd wilkinson	*16s 2d*
To the [. . . ..]	*3s*
To mathew wilkinson	*12d*
To the church	*20s*

To [] baxter	*40s*
To Elizabeth Jackson	*21s 18d*
To marye denny	*20s*
To Isabell Lowish	*13s 4d*
To Rychard fearan	*£5*
To Roland denny	*10s*
To henrye denny	*4s*
To heughe gybson	*£3-6s-2d*
To Leonard machell	*26s-8d*
To henrye denneson	*36s*
To John hotblack	*17s*
To John Robinson	*16s*
	Summa £32 – 3s – 7d

John Airey left an estate which had more liabilities (£32 3s 7d) than assets (£31 10s). His will illustrates the widespread practice where friends and neighbours were willing to lend money in the days before an easily available banking system allowed people to survive economically hard times.

It is apparent from the valuation of the will of Henry Holme of Flakehow, dated 1670, that times were more prosperous and that Flakehow was one of the largest farms in the dale. The will is complex but still accentuates the value of simple items such as ash ladders and tools for gathering wood and peat. There is also reference to the continued care of the chapel and the need to provide for a minister.

Will of Henry Holme 1670

In the name of god amen I Henry Holme of Flakehow in the parish of Bampton and county of Westmorland, yeoman, being weak and sick in body, but of perfect rememberance (I blesse the lord for itt) doe make this my last will and Testament in manner and forme as followeth And first I commend my soul into the handes of allmighty god my maker, hopeing in and through the righteousness of Jesus Christ my most mercifull Saviour and gracious redeemer to be made inheritour of eternall blisse: my body I Committ to the dust from whence it was taken, namely to buryed in the parish church of Bampton, assuredly beleiving that by the mighty power of Christ Jesus itt shall bee raised incorruptible with

my soul to enjoy everlasting joy: And as for the goodes which the lord in mercy hath lent me: I give and dispose of them in manner and forme as followeth. And first I doe heerby revoke and make void all former wills made by me either in words or writeinge
Item I give to my wife Agnes, and my eldest son William Holme and my son George Holme thirty of the best ewes which they shall Chuse in my flock to be equally devided amongst them
Item I give to my wife Agnes, and my son Henry Holme and my son Geore Holme thirty of the west weathers, which they shall Chuse in my flock, to be equally divided amongst them.
Item I give to my son Henry Holme other ten weathers of the best which he shall Chuse after the Choise of the former thirty be made as abovesaid.
Item I give to my son George tenne of the best twinter weathers and five weather hoggs, such as he shall Chuse after the Chouses abovesaid be made
Item I give to my said sons George & Henry fore of the best twinter gimmers which they shall make Choise of.
Item I give to my Son in Law William Cowperthwaite, tenne of the best twinter gimmers, which he shall Chuse in my flock
Item I give to Agnes the daughter of the said William Cowperthwait four of the best gimmer hoggs which her father shall Chuse for her in my flock
Item I give to William & Henry the sons of my oldest son William Holme two gimmer hoggs to be Chosen by their father after the Chouses aforesd be made.
Item I give to my son William Holmes all my plough geare provided my wife hve the use of them dureing her life, and that my sd son William doe uphold & keep them [..........]
Item I give to my sed son William the great Arke which standes in the Cellar; and the [........] which stands upon the loft
Item I give to my son Henry Holme the ark which standes in the barne, and the [................] pewter dish of which I have.
Item I give to my son George Holme my dun'd mare and the

cupboard which ………… The fire house with my tarckney saddle and the better of my …
Item I give to my wife Agnes and my son George Six of the best kine, or heffers, which I have.
Item I give to my wife aforesd, and my son George, the Rcken Crook, tongues, hack, gavelock axe or hattchett, and all the hay and Corne in the barne, all the bedding: and bedstocks in the house.
Item I give to my son Henry Holme the bedstocke which standes in the Chamber
Item I give to my son Henry three stone of woll, such as my son Geore shall Chuse for him out of all my woll for making beddcloathes
Item I give to every one of the Children of my son Henry Holme one gimmar hog.
Item I give to the Chappell stock of Mardail Seven Shillings; to be pautt forward with thirteen shillings which allready is in my hand of the said stock: And if the inhabitants within the said Chappelrie can agree to purchase land with the Chappelstock that the Crop, or rent of the said land may be disposed of for payment of the Curates wages. Then I give twenty shillings money towards the said purchase; to be payed by my executors within one month after the purchase made. Provided if not such purchase be made, then this Legacy is to be void.
Item I give twenty stone of woll to my wife, and my son George
Item I give one stone of woll to my sister Elizabeth Cowperthwait of Kentmeer
Item I give half a stone of woll to the wife of Thomas Yates of Waters
Item I give to my son George Holme tenn ewes , such as he shall Chuse in all my flock after the making of the Choses abovesaid.
Item I give to my said son George soe many oaken boards as he shall Chuse about my house to make him a Chist.
Item I give to my son George Holme one table which standes n my son William's house

Item I give to my son Wiliam the table which standes in my house
Item I give to Thomas Hoggart my man servant five shilling
Item. I give to Henry Lowes my servant one shilling
Item I give all my Sledges, barrowes, spades & such utensills as belong to getting of fewill, and one ash=ladder to my wife, and my son George
Item I give to my son Henry two sides of Aspen wood, to make him a ladder
Item I give to my son George all the Tar and sheep sakve with all the vessells, kitts, gallons, or Dosterills belonging to them with one fell staff, or shepherds staff.
Lastly, all the rest of my goodes moveable and iunmoveable of what nature or quality soever and in whose handes soever they be, I give & bequeath to my son Henry Holme, my son George Holme: and my son in law William Cowperthwaith,whom I nominate joynt executor of this my last will & Testament. In Wittnesse whereof I have heerunto sett my hand & seal the four....... Of January Anno Domini 1669
Henry Holme

Signed Sealed & declared in presence of mark & seal
William Holme de Groave Bray
Rt Stewardson

Memorandum that before the wittnesses to this will Henry Holme the testator did declare that it was his minde to give to his wife Agnes thirty shillings thirty shillings which Margaret Denny of Wallmrgate was oweing to him And that this should be annexed to his will.
Testamet hoc [witnessed here]
William Holme de Groave bray [mark]Henry Holme his [mark]
And John Holme de Groave bray [mark]

The son of Henry Holme, also called Henry, made his will in 1721 when he was residing at Chapel Hill and described as Yeoman. The will illustrates a slight change of style. It is more to the point and contains less preamble but still begins with the reference to the soul and body. It is interesting to note that there is very little remaining after the estate is settled. The total of goods from the inventory is £55 4s 0d, debts and funeral expenses amounted to £51 13s 0d, leaving a 'real sume' of £03 11s 0d.

Will of Henry Holme 1721

In the name of God Amen, the 25th day of Aprill Anno Domini 1721.

I Henry Holme of Chappel Hill in Mardale in the County of Westmorland Yeoman, being weake in body, but of a right disposeing mind doe make this my last Will and testament wherever is confirmed my last Will and testament in manner following. ffirst I bequeath my soul to God that gave it, and my body to the ground decently to be interred by my executors and my temporal estate I dispose as followeth

Imprimis I give to my daughter Jane five shillings

Item I give to my daughter Isabel Dennyson tenn shillings

Item I give to my daughter Ann Ayrey tenn shillings, and to her sonn Henry tenn shillings

Item I give to my daughter [Annas?] twenty shillings

Item I give to my daughter Ffrances Tenn shillings

Item I give to my daughter Margaret tenn shillings

Item I give to my sonn Richard tenn Shillings

Item I give to my sonn Thomas two pounds and tenn shillings

Item I give to my wife Jane Holme five pounds

Item all the residue and remainder of my Goods and Chattels moveable and not moveable, Debts, credits and demands and personal Estate whatsoever I give and bequeath to my sonn John Holme, whom I doe hereby make constitute ordain and appoint Sole Executor of this my last Will and testament. hee paying my legacyes as above, and satisfying and dischargiing my just devts and funeral expences. In Wittnesse whereof I have hereunto sett my hand and seal the day and year above written.

Signed, sealed, published and declared in presence of
John Holme sworne
William Holme *Henry Holme mark*

Henry Holme H
Probate granted Appleby 16th Dec 1721

Inventory of Henry Holme 1721

A true and perfect inventory of the Goods and Chattels of Henry Holme of Chappel Hill in the parish of Shapp, lately deceased made and taken this Ninth day of May A.D. 1721 by us whose names are underwritten

Imprimis	£ s d
Purse & apparrell	01 10 00
Bedding and Bedsteads	00 15 00
Sacks, poaks & Winding cloth	00 08 00
Brass and Pewter	01 18 00
Potts, Pottles & Wooden bessels	00 11 00
Arks Chests & Cupboard & Table and Books	02 12 00
Crook Tongs Brandrith GridIron Bakboard & Chafyng dish and frying pann	00 05 00
Plow and plow gear and all other utensils of husbandry	01 00 00
Chairs & Formes Wheeles and Cards and loose Wood	00 06 00
Salve Kitts & tarr	00 06 00
Ropes	00 03 00
Wool	00 10 00
Corn meale and Flesh	01 00 00
Beasts young and old	18 00 00
Horses young and old	06 00 00
Sheep of all sorts	20 00 00
Sume	£55 04 00
Deduct Debts owing by the deceasd & Funerall expenses ————	£51 13 00
Real Sume	£03 11 00

Approved at Appleby
10th December 1721

Sworne John Holme
Sworne John Holme
Apprisors: John Holme

William Holme

From the beginning of the eighteenth century wills included more bequests of actual money. Isabel Holme of Wheltar 1704, Miles Holme of Bowderthwaite 1707, John Tinkler of Measand 1716 and William Holme of Grove Brae 1717, all leave sums of money ranging from one shilling to twenty shillings to various family members and servants.

Margaret Wright, a widow of Seal Green in Measand, was farming on her own account according to the inventory of her goods and chattels valued on the 16th March 1729:

Inventory of Margaret Wright

A true & perfect Inventory of the goods & chattles of Margrett Wright widdow, late of Seal Green in Measand Within the parish aforsaid, Apraised by Richard Holme of Brownsike & John Holme of Sandhill, this sixteenth day of March A:D: 1729

	£ s d
Imprimis purse & aparel	*5 16 00*
Chests & household stuff	*1 00 00*
Bedding & bed steads	*1 10 00*
Meal malts & victuals	*0 10 00*
Corn of all sorts	*1 16 00*
Hay	*0 8 00*
Beasts	*4 00 00*
Sheep	*5 5 00*
Peats & poultry	*00 1 00*
Mannure	*00 2 06*
Wool	*00 5 00*
Crook & tongs stools & chairs	*00 1 00*
	20 15 00
Funeral Expenses	*01 5 00*
Totall	*19 10 00*

Richard Holmes sworn
John Holme sworn Appraisers

When Thomas Greenhow of Riggindale made his will in 1779 the format had become more secular in nature with bequests of money rather than goods and chattels, which in the case of Thomas Greenhow were left as a whole to his eldest son Thomas.

Will of Thomas Greenhow 1779

In the name of God, amen. I Thomas Greenhow the older of Riggindale in the parish of Bampton, being of sound and perfect mind and memory do make this my last Will and Testament in manner and form following, that is to say First I give and bequeath unto my son William Greenhow the sum of twenty pounds and also to each of his children I give the sum of five shillings. Also to my Daughter Elizabeth the wife of JamesHutchinson I give the sum of £4. Also to her two Daughters, to each of them the sum of five shillings. Also I give to my daughter Agnes the wife of Gerrard Huck the sum of four pounds; also to each of her childer I give the sum of five shillings. Also to my daughter E....y the wife of William Dobson I give the sum of two pounds and two shillings, and also to her daughter Elizabeth I give the sum of five shillings. Also to my grandson John Greenhow of Riggindale I give the sum of five shillings. All the residue and remainder of my goods, Chattels, Credits and personal Estate whatsoever I give and bequeath unto my son Thomas Greenhow whom I make and appoint the sole executor of this my last Will, repaying my just Debts and funeral Expences and also paying and discharging the above named legacies at the end of twelve kalender months next after my decease. In witnes whereof I have hereunto set my hand and seal this twenty sixth day of April in the year of our Lord one thousand seven hundred seventy and nine. I revoke and cancel all former Wills by me made.

Thomas Greenhow his mark

Signed, sealed and declared to be his last Will and Testament by the above named Thomas Greenhow in the presence of us William Hayton his mark John Holme sworne.

Proved May 31st 1779

The will of George Hayton made in 1816 illustrates, as is other cases, the intermingling of local families through marriage.

Will of George Hayton

In the name of God, Amen. I George Hayton of Mardale in the parish of Shap in the County of Westmorland, Yeoman, being of sound Mind and Memory and mindful of my Mortality, Do this Eighteenth day of March in the year of our Lord 1814, make and publish this my last Will and Testament in manner following. FIRST I give and bequeath unto my Daughter Agnes Rawes, wife of Gerard Rawes of Mardale aforesaid, the sum of Forty Pounds, to be paid unto her at the Expiration of one year after my Decease. ALSO I give and bequeath unto my Grandson George Mawson of Mardale aforesaid all that my Flock of Heath going Sheep whatsoever and wheresoever to be delivered to him immediately after my decease. All the rest and residue of my Personal Estate and Effects, Goods and Chattels whatsoever and wheresoever and of what nature kind and Quality soever the same may be, and hereinbefore given and disposed of {after payment of my Debts, Legacies and Funeral Expences) I do give and bequeath to my eldest daughter Jane Hayton, her Executors Administrators and Assigns, to and for her and their own use and benefit absolutely And I do hereby constitute and appoint my said Daughter Jane Hayton sole Executrix of this my last Will and Testament. IN WITNESS whereof I have hereunto set my had and seal the Day and year first above written. George Hayton his mark X and Seal XX. SIGNED sealed published and declared by the said Testator as and for his last Will and Testament in our presence who at his request in his presence and in the presence of each other have subscribed our names as witnesses thereto. John Bowstead, Gerard Rawes.

Effects under £100.

Proved by Jane Hayton of Mardale, Spinster, the sole Executrix, the 2nd July 1816

By 1872 the Holme Family were well established as the Kings of Mardale owning an estate of several farms and an Inn. Their wealth and status is reflected in the will of John Holme, father of Hugh Parker Holme, known as the last King of Mardale.

Will of John Holme 1872 (extract)

This is the last Will and Testament of me John Holme of Chapel Hill Mardale in the County of Westmorland, Yeoman. I give to my dear Wife Mary Holme an Annuity and yearly sum of Sixty pounds payable by two equal half yearly payments the first payment to begin and be made on the expiration of six Calendar months after my decease And I declare that the yearly sum of Thirthy five pounds part of the said Annuity shall be charged upon and issuing and payable out of the real Estate herinafter devised to my Eldest Son Hugh Parker Holme and the yearly sum of Twenty five pounds remaining part therof shall be charged upon and issuing and payable out of the real Estate hereinafter devised to my Younger Son Thomas Joseph Holme And I give to my said wife powers of entry and distress for recovering the said sums respectively in like manner as if the same had been rents reserved on a Common Lease I also give to my said Wife the use of all my household goods and furniture plates, Linen, china and other household Effects for and during her life And from and after her decease I give the same to my said Son Hugh Parker Holme absolutely. I also give to my said Wife the use of my Dwelling House at Chapel Hill aforesaid for and during her life I give to my said Son Thomas Joseph Holme my Estate or Farm called Green Head as now occupied by Robert Clark as tennant Together with the Sheep let therewith, also the Sheep let with my Estate or Tenement called Brackenhowe Also my Estate or Farm called Goosemire including the Allotments on Mardale Green which are situate on the East Side of Mardale Green Beck (but not including Brackenhowe Tenement or Rig Side and Dudgrig Allotment) Also my two fields called Dubbin Acre and Arnold Green now in my own occupation and situate on the East side of the said Beck. I give and devise All the rest residue, and remainder of my real Estate unto my said Son Hugh Parker Holme his heirs and assigns I give all the rest residue and remainder of my personal Estate and Effects Subject to the payment of my debts and funeral and Testamentary Expences to my said Son Hugh Parker Holme absolutely And in case the sum shall be insufficient for the payment of my said debts and funeral and testamentary expenses I charge three fifths of the deficiency on the real Estate hereinbefore devised to my said Son Hugh Parker Holme and the remaining two fifths on the real Estate hereinbefore devised to my said Son Thomas Joseph Holme And whereas I expect that my daughter Anne Maria Holme will be amply provided for by her Grandfather Mr Benjamin Grisdale Now I declare that in case she shall not at his death inherit from him or become entitled under his Will to an annual Income during her life or property real or personal producing an annual income of Twenty pounds I give to her the Legacy of One thousand pounds.

The wills contained in this chapter give an illustration of the life's achievements of the people of Mardale. In the sixteenth and seventeenth centuries everything a person owned was vital only to their survival. There is no trace of surplus or items of luxury. With the exception of those occupied by the Holme family, the farms and cottages were tenanted so there was no property to bequeath.

In the 18th century there is evidence of a more prosperous way of life. The wealth of the Holme family was building and sustaining several branches on their estate and the amalgamation of smaller farms into bigger and more sustainable units provided a better living, creating a more monetary society, although sheep were still the most valued item.

Wills of the 19th century are more akin to modern standards. However, whilst the will of John Holme 1872 suggests that he was a man of considerable wealth, those of the tenant farmers would suggest that life in this remote dale was still a matter of hand to mouth.

Glossary

almery: a kind of closed cupboard for storage
arke: chest for storing animal feed to protect it from vermin
bakboard: a wooden board used for rolling out dough
bedstock: a bed frame
bedding: blankets etc, vital to life before central heating
bill, billhook: a long narrow blade with a wooden handle, for cutting vegetation
brandreth: an iron trivet
bushell: eight gallons (dry weight), a measure, typically of oats, etc.
chafing dish: a dish raised on legs, used to cook away from the direct flame
Chapel stock: donation to the upkeep of the church
chest: used for storage, anything from tools and feed to clothes
chist, chiste, chyst etc: a chest, see above
crokes: probably rattencrooks, see below
gavelock: a crowbar
gimmer: a female sheep, could be a lamb, hogg or ewe according to its age
gridiron: a metal plate with parallel bars for grilling meat or fish
gylefat: a large vat used for fermentation in the brewing process
hogg: a young sheep, older than a lamb, but not yet had own lamb
husbandrygear: equipment for farming, looking after the livestock
kye: cow or heifer
Lady Day: 25th March. This used to be the last day of the year, but New Year's Day was changed to 1st January in 1752. It had importance as being the day on which yearly contracts began and finished, so has special relevance for tenant farmers. It now marks the end of the first quarter of the year.
Lammas Day: 1st August. A medieval quarter day, with Whitsuntide (the 7th Sunday after Easter), then Lammas, then Martinmas (11th November), finally Candlemas (2nd February). In older days, a reckoning-up day for accounts

Manure: manure, a valuable fertiliser!
Martinmas: 11th November (see Lammas Day)
Michalmas: 29th September. Foretells the coming of Autumn and shorter days
netherend: lower end
plowgear: ploughing equipment
puder: pewter. Pewter dishes were much more expensive than wood
rattencrook, rakencroke: the iron frame over the fire from which hung the cooking pots.
sheep salve: a mix of tar and rancid butter rubbed into the wool to discourage parasites. Used up to the beginning of the 20th century. A long and tiring job.
sleddes: sledges. Much more use in the valley than wheels!
St Andrews Day: 30th November. Patron saint of Scotland.
stryke, stirk: a bovine between a calf and an adult in age
tar: used for all sorts, including the making of sheep salve, see above
tup: male sheep used for breeding
twinter: has lived as long as two winters!
wargeare: weapons
wether, weather: neutered male sheep
Whye, whie: a heifer, a young (female) cow
yow: a ewe, adult female sheep

Chapter 9

The Kings of Mardale

THE HOLME FAMILY

The Holmes were the dominant family in Mardale for 700 years. While he was writing 'Shappe in Bygone Days', Joseph Whiteside was given access to several documents in the possession of Mrs Elizabeth Holme. He believed some of them to be copies of older documents. All contained slightly varying accounts and one, supposedly the oldest document, tells the story as follows:

'In they year of the Incarnation of our blessed Lord and Saviour one thousand 67, at the time that William the conqueror brought his army into Brittain's Isle many lords and Gentlemen came along with them. Amongst the rest was a certain gentleman out of the Country of Stockholme a valiant young squire whose name was John being one of very handsome conduct and being taken notice of by the General himself who made him a captain in his army. When the invasion was ended and all feuds and disturbances were quietly settled and this notable Conqueror fixed upon the throne of England, this worthy Prince forthwith rewarded his soldiers with everyone an estate for their famous valour and trusty manhood.

All his officers and men of note in the first place were taken notice of.

This same John, from Stockholme being of an ancient family being the 9th or 10th of that family or name, was by this great prince settled on an Estate in Yorkshire of the yearly value of 350 pounds, deriving his name from the place of his nativity.

In the county of York he lived peaceably for the term of 35 years having several sons and daughters. After his decease his eldest son William succeeded him who lived after him 40 years leaving a son whose name was Richard, he died after he had lived 37 years; his son Henry succeeded him enjoying the estate 23 years until the reign of King John in the year 1203.

This same died and left a son whom he called Hugh Holme. This

Hugh lived upon the Domain quietly until the decree came out from the King.'[1]

The decree from the King concerned Hugh's alleged involvement in the Canterbury plot. Another of the documents continues:

'It is well known that in this reign there were several disputes and quarrels between the King and his subjects and in the year 1209 King John was engaged in a very serious dispute with some Monks of Canterbury and other Ecclesiastics and finding that several of his lay subjects were likely to join the clergy, he endeavoured to prevent such as he most suspected: from some he required hostages, their friends or children, to be put into hands as pledges of their loyalty: some he imprisoned some fled: among these last was Hugh Holme who then represented the family and feeling himself liable to be questioned he thought better to fly rather than starve in Jail or perhaps loose his head, taking his journey northward he chanced to light into Mardale, which being surrounded by high mountains and these in a great measure covered with wood he thought proper to stay for a while, and was civilly entertained by an old man near the middle of the dale who proved a faithful friend to him and directed him to a place where he might retire when he chose to be in secret: the place is near the foot of a great rock called Riggindale Crag and still retains the name of Hugh's cave.'[2]

HUGH DE HOLME ARRNIN AT MARDALE:: FROM A SEAL FORMERLY IN SHAP ABBEY. CIRCA. 1214::

Whatever truth this legend was based on, it is obvious that the Holmes were in Mardale from a very early date. There were several branches of the family living in Mardale in the second part of the sixteenth century and their name was linked with most of the dwellings through the ensuing years, the main one being Chapel Hill which would suggest a family settled for many years in the place.

Through the centuries the family used Norman style Christian names, William, Henry, Richard, Myles and Thomas, John and Hugh. From arriving in Mardale until the later years of the 18th century the family were widely represented in the valley. Thereafter the family declined in numbers for various

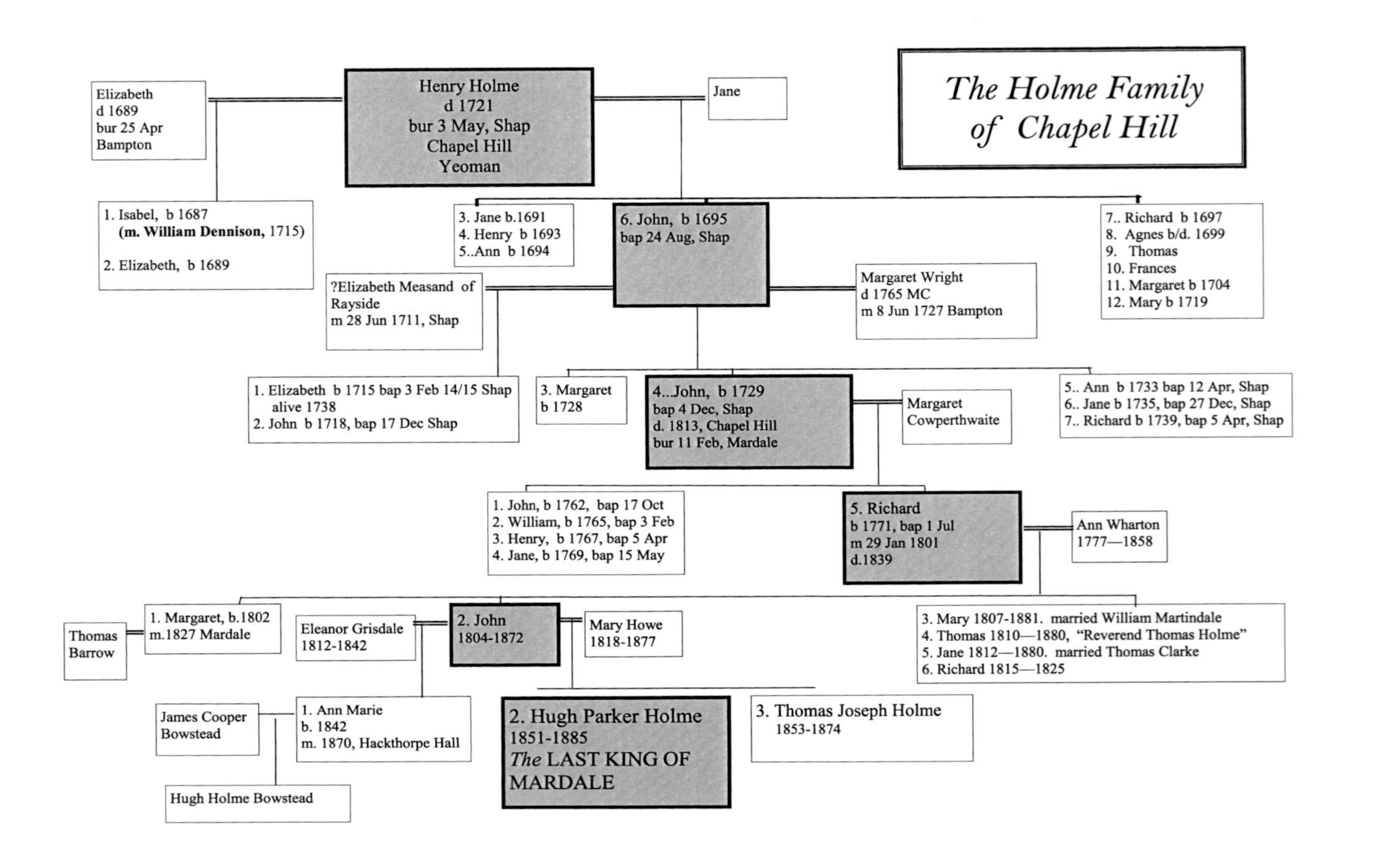
The Holme Family of Chapel Hill
Elizabeth d 1689 bur 25 Apr Bampton
Henry Holme d 1721 bur 3 May, Shap Chapel Hill Yeoman
Jane
1. Isabel, b 1687 (m. William Dennison, 1715)
2. Elizabeth, b 1689
3. Jane b.1691
4. Henry b 1693
5..Ann b 1694
6. John, b 1695 bap 24 Aug, Shap
7.. Richard b 1697
8. Agnes b/d. 1699
9. Thomas
10. Frances
11. Margaret b 1704
12. Mary b 1719
?Elizabeth Measand of Rayside m 28 Jun 1711, Shap
Margaret Wright d 1765 MC m 8 Jun 1727 Bampton
1. Elizabeth b 1715 bap 3 Feb 14/15 Shap alive 1738
2. John b 1718, bap 17 Dec Shap
3. Margaret b 1728
4...John, b 1729 bap 4 Dec, Shap d. 1813, Chapel Hill bur 11 Feb, Mardale
Margaret Cowperthwaite
5.. Ann b 1733 bap 12 Apr, Shap
6.. Jane b 1735, bap 27 Dec, Shap
7.. Richard b 1739, bap 5 Apr, Shap
1. John, b 1762, bap 17 Oct
2. William, b 1765, bap 3 Feb
3. Henry, b 1767, bap 5 Apr
4. Jane, b 1769, bap 15 May
5. Richard b 1771, bap 1 Jul m 29 Jan 1801 d.1839
Ann Wharton 1777—1858
Thomas Barrow
1. Margaret, b.1802 m.1827 Mardale
Eleanor Grisdale 1812-1842
2. John 1804-1872
Mary Howe 1818-1877
3. Mary 1807-1881. married William Martindale
4. Thomas 1810—1880, "Reverend Thomas Holme"
5. Jane 1812—1880. married Thomas Clarke
6. Richard 1815—1825
James Cooper Bowstead
1. Ann Marie b. 1842 m. 1870, Hackthorpe Hall
Hugh Holme Bowstead
2. Hugh Parker Holme 1851-1885 The LAST KING OF MARDALE
3. Thomas Joseph Holme 1853-1874

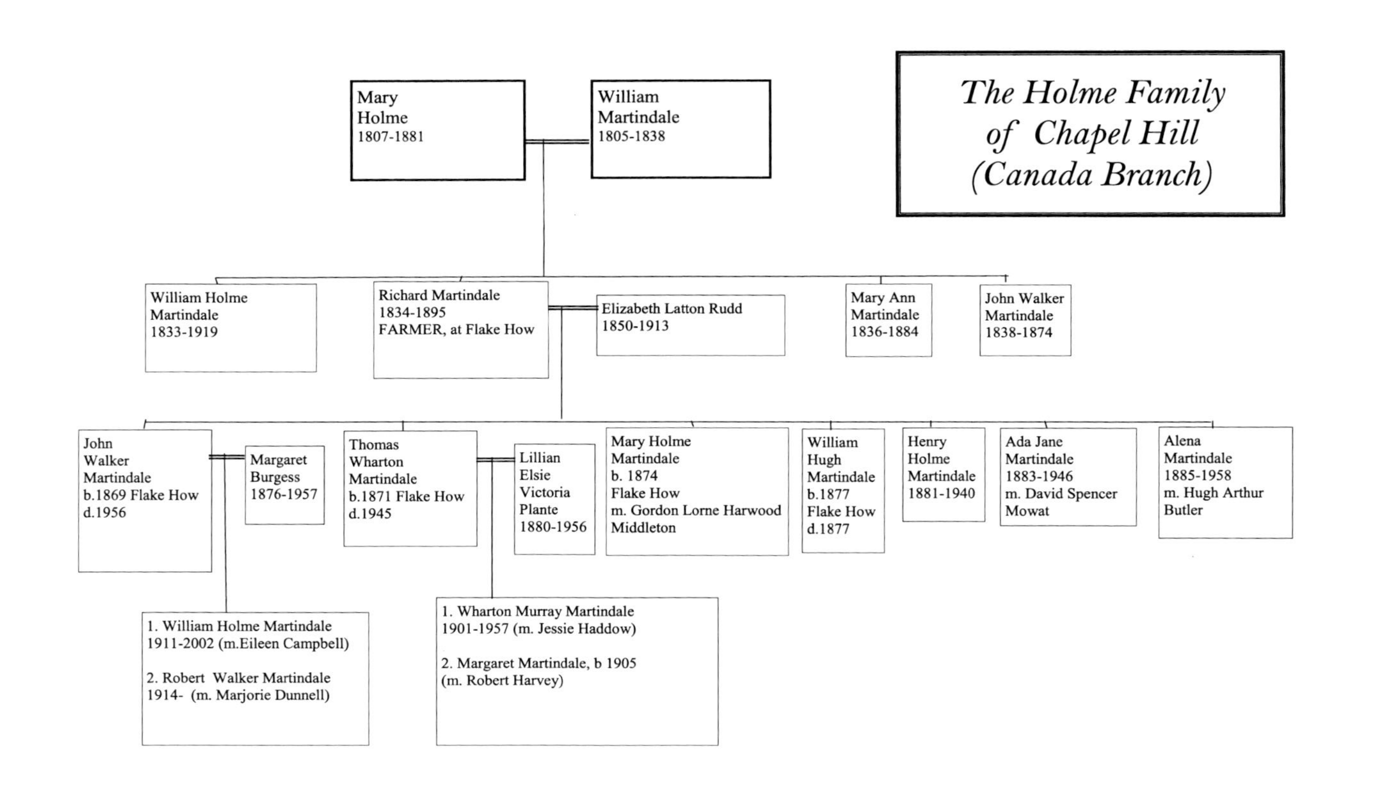

The Holme Family
of Chapel Hill
(Canada Branch)
Mary
Holme
1807-1881
William
Martindale
1805-1838
William Holme
Martindale
1833-1919
Richard Martindale
1834-1895
FARMER, at Flake How
Elizabeth Latton Rudd
1850-1913
Mary Ann
Martindale
1836-1884
John Walker
Martindale
1838-1874
John
Walker
Martindale
b.1869 Flake How
d.1956
Margaret
Burgess
1876-1957
Thomas
Wharton
Martindale
b.1871 Flake How
d.1945
Lillian
Elsie
Victoria
Plante
1880-1956
Mary Holme
Martindale
b. 1874
Flake How
m. Gordon Lorne Harwood
Middleton
William
Hugh
Martindale
b.1877
Flake How
d.1877
Henry
Holme
Martindale
1881-1940
Ada Jane
Martindale
1883-1946
m. David Spencer
Mowat
Alena
Martindale
1885-1958
m. Hugh Arthur
Butler
1. William Holme Martindale
1911-2002 (m.Eileen Campbell)
2. Robert Walker Martindale
1914- (m. Marjorie Dunnell)
1. Wharton Murray Martindale
1901-1957 (m. Jessie Haddow)
2. Margaret Martindale, b 1905
(m. Robert Harvey)

Mrs Holme, Hugh's mother

Hugh Parker Holme

Manny Boustead, nephew of Hugh Holme

reasons and when Richard and his wife Ann nee Wharton built the new house at Chapel Hill they were the only Holmes left there. By then the family had become local aristocracy owning a considerable estate based on Chapel Hill. Over the years the family became known as the Kings of Mardale.

The boys of the family benefited from the education provided at Measand Grammar School and many of them left the valley for university. William, brother to Richard, became a vicar. His nephew, Thomas, son of Richard and Ann Holme, followed him into the ministry and eventually returned to the living of Mardale, where he died in 1880.

Another son of Richard and Ann Holme, William, was described as Medical Practitioner and Member of the Royal College of Surgeons in 1851 when he was in practice in Windermere. They also had a daughter Ann who became Mrs William Martindale.

The last to be called the King of Mardale was Hugh Parker Holme, son of John and Mary Holme and the grandson of Richard and Ann. He was educated at St Bees along with his brother, Thomas Joseph. Hugh took up the running of the estate at Chapel Hill and became a noted breeder of Herdwick sheep, gaining premier honours at local shows and at the Royal Show. The direct line of decent ended with Hugh's death in 1885, at the age of 34.

His only brother, Thomas Joseph, had predeceased him in

1872, aged only 21. Anne Marie, his sister who had married James C. Boustead of Hackthorpe Hall also died in 1891, aged 48 and without heirs as her only son, Hugh Holme (Manny Boustead), had died in 1886 at the age of 15.

THE MARTINDALE FAMILY

William Martindale was born in Kendal in 1807 and married Mary Holme, the daughter of Richard and Ann Holme of Chapel Hill, at Mardale Church in 1832. They had four children – William Holme born in 1833, Richard born in 1834, Mary Ann born in 1836 and John Walker born in 1838. This John Walker died at Mardale in 1874, aged 36.

John Walker Martindale held by his grandmother Anne Latton Martindale with parents Elizabeth Latton Martindale and Richard Martindale

An account appeared in a Kendal newspaper giving details of the mysterious disappearance of William Martindale of Flakehow who, according to the report, was never seen again. However, there is more to the story. William died or vanished sometime between 1838 and 1840 leaving a widow and four very young children, named above. If he did live with his family at Flakehow it was for a very brief period. His son, Richard, went to live at Chapel Hill with his grandfather and uncle when his father died. Mary, William's widow, lived with her brother William Holme, MRCS, a Medical Practitioner at Ambleside and worked as his housekeeper. After William the doctor married, Mary moved to live at Greenbank, Patterdale where she is recorded living with her daughter, Mary Ann aged 24 and her son Richard, aged 26, who was visiting from Mardale with John Greenhow, probably the curate, in the 1861 census. In 1871 she was living at Deer How, Patterdale with another son, John Walker, a Medical Practitioner. Mary died in 1881.

Mary Ann Martindale

It was Richard who farmed at Flakehow. He married Elizabeth Latton Rudd at Mardale Church in September 1868. They had sons, John Walker, Thomas Wharton, William Hugh (who died at birth) and Henry Holme, and daughters Mary and Ada Jane, all born at Flakehow. They left Mardale around 1885. Another daughter, Alena, was born at Levens. In the 1891 census they were at One Cote Farm, Leek in Staffordshire.

On 25th February 1892 Richard, Ann and all their family sailed from Liverpool to Halifax on the SS Mongolian, their final destination being Victoria, British Columbia. Richard died in Victoria BC on 24th February 1895 shortly after their arrival. Elizabeth, his wife, died in 1913 in Parksville, BC. John Walker Martindale died at Victoria BC in 1956. Thomas Wharton Martindale married in Canada and died in 1945 in Nanaimo, BC. His sister, Mary Holme Martindale, who married Gorden Lorne Middleton in Canada, died in Nanaimo BC in 1951. Henry Holme Martindale died in Nanaimo BC in 1940. Ada Jane who married David Spencer Mowat in Canada died at Victoria BC in 1946. Alena, who married Hugh Arthur Butler in Canada, died in Namaino BC in June 1958. A large number of the descendants of Richard Martindale and Elizabeth Latton Rudd still live in Canada. Thomas Wharton Martindale returned to Mardale for a visit in 1903 and gave a talk inviting others to follow him to Canada. There was a big demand for people willing to emigrate at this time, and it is interesting to note that when Thomas W Martindale returned to Canada on the SS Kensington in 1906 two names from Westmorland appeared on the shipping list beside him.

Other Mardale Families

'From time immemorial'

Shap Church registers give the first records of occupation of Mardale. Examination of these records reveals that as few as eight to ten family names were present in the valley when the registers began in 1559. These names were also to be found in adjacent valleys of Martindale, Patterdale, Sleddale, Cawdale and Kentmere.

From time immemorial these families had populated the Westmorland 'dales' when the mountain passes were the highways and main routes of communication, migrating back and forward between them. Many of these families, the Jacksons for instance, were well established in Mardale in the late sixteenth century as up to four branches were living there at that time.

The movement was continuous as families sought better and more profitable holdings to lease. For example in some cases they would leave a farm in Mardale to go to a better one in Bampton but would return when another became available in Mardale. These families populated Mardale for the next two hundred years. Among them were Jacksons, Watsons, Dennysons, Wrights, Robinsons, Richardsons, Haytons, Baxters and Greens. Gradually they all disappeared from the valley.

The following families all fit into this category.

THE KITCHING FAMILY

Thomas Kitching was born in Kentmere c1810 and was the son of William and Mary Kitching, of Hallow Bank, Kentmere. In 1850 Thomas with his wife Jane and their family moved from Kentmere to Sandhills in Measand. Shortly after they moved to Measand Beck Farm. On his marriage to Elizabeth Bousfield of Kirkby Stephen in 1873, William, eldest son of Thomas and Mary, took up the tenancy of Sandhills. When Thomas died William inherited the title of the Mardale Boatman. The position involved looking after the boathouse with the boats and fishing equipment kept there for the use of the large fishing parties brought to the lake by Lord Lonsdale. When William died in 1901 aged fifty years the following appeared in the church magazine:

'It is with deep regret that we have to record the death of one who has lived the whole of his life in this valley. We refer to William Kitching son of the late Thomas and Jane Kitching of Measand Farm.

The boathouse

Both father and son were 'boatmen' on the lake under the Earl, and were well known to all trout fishers in the two counties. The father died about ten years ago, but the mother is still with us. The sympathy of all will go out to the mother, widow and children of our departed friend.'[3]

William and Elizabeth had fifteen children. It is said that he took their names from the visitors to Lowther Castle who fished on the lake. However some were family names and names of others in the valley, some of whom may have stood as godparents. The children were named as follows:

Ada Jane Marie 1873
Janet Augusta Louisa 1875
Tom Harrison Bousfield 1876 (his third name was from his mother's family)
Florence Winifred Hunter 1878
Gladys Waistell Lennex 1880
William Theodore Barron 1881
Lowther Lonsdale Liddell 1883
Brunskill Hayes Bland 1884
Hugh Harvey Hayton 1886

Arthur Hassel Duncan 1887
Noble Boustead Holmes 1889
Selina Rose Parker 1891
Albert Ashington Donald Sykes 1892
Mabel Gertrude W 1893
Elsie Violet CFM 1897

The Kitching family haymaking

Hugh and William emigrated to Canada in about 1904, though William later returned to Cumbria. Hugh settled in Montreal and had six sons. Arthur, Albert, Selina, and Noble went to Canada in 1910. Noble returned to Mardale. Arthur died in Toronto, Albert was killed at the battle of the Somme and Lowther was killed at the Dardenelles. Tom was wounded whilst on army service in about 1917, but lived until 1966 and died within a month of his ninetieth birthday. Thomas Harrison Kitching stayed in Mardale and continued to farm at Measand.

There are many descendants of Thomas and Jane Kitching still living Cumbria.

THE JACKSON FAMILY

Church records in the late medieval period show that there was a large family of this name in Mardale, namely in Naddle and in Guerness. The name was also widespread in the neighbouring valleys of Swindale and Sleddale and also in Shap. They

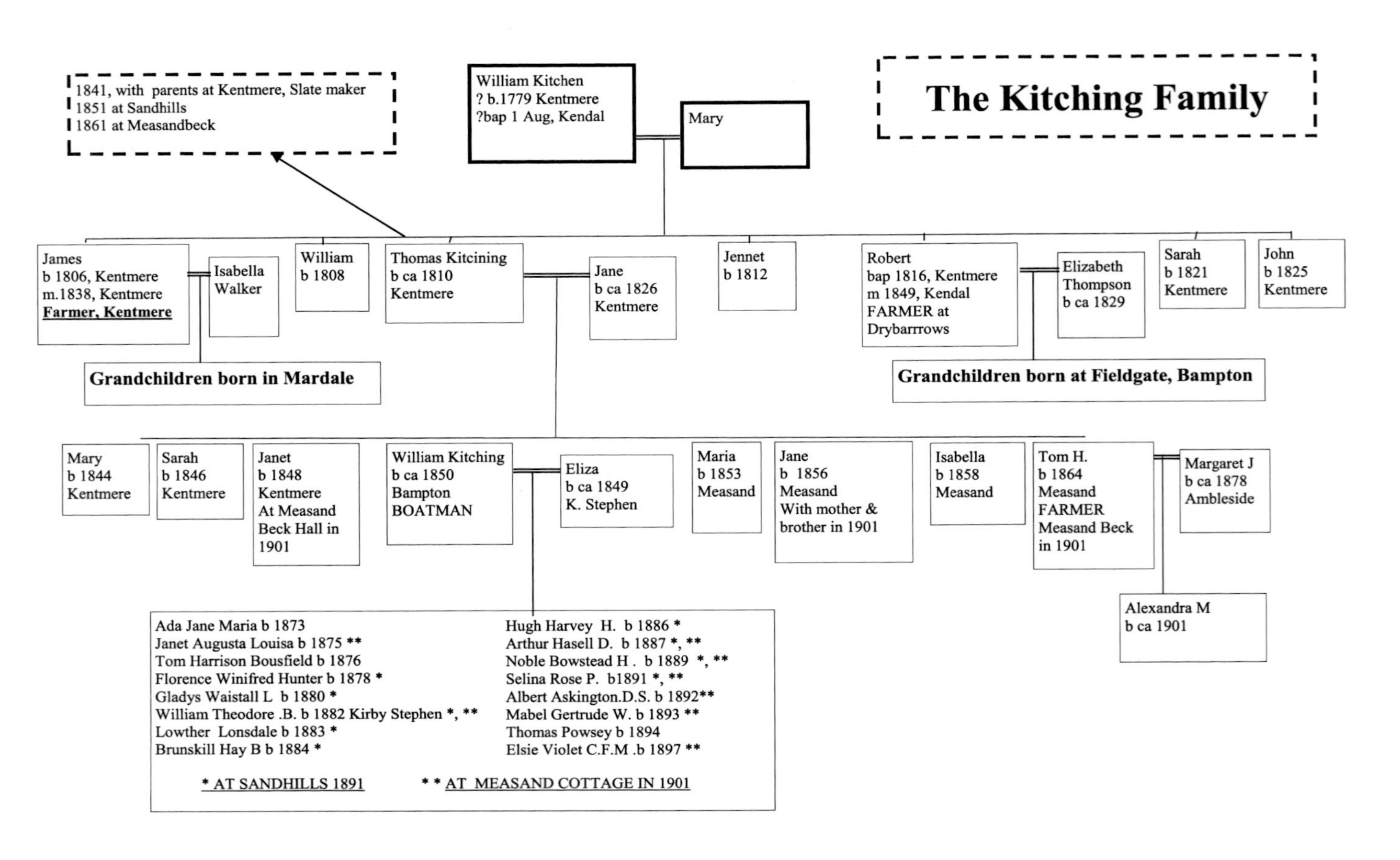
The Kitching Family
1841, with parents at Kentmere, Slate maker
1851 at Sandhills
1861 at Measandbeck
William Kitchen
? b.1779 Kentmere
?bap 1 Aug, Kendal
Mary
James
b 1806, Kentmere
m.1838, Kentmere
Farmer, Kentmere
Isabella
Walker
William
b 1808
Thomas Kitcining
b ca 1810
Kentmere
Jane
b ca 1826
Kentmere
Jennet
b 1812
Robert
bap 1816, Kentmere
m 1849, Kendal
FARMER at
Drybarrrows
Elizabeth
Thompson
b ca 1829
Sarah
b 1821
Kentmere
John
b 1825
Kentmere
Grandchildren born in Mardale
Grandchildren born at Fieldgate, Bampton
Mary
b 1844
Kentmere
Sarah
b 1846
Kentmere
Janet
b 1848
Kentmere
At Measand
Beck Hall in
1901
William Kitching
b ca 1850
Bampton
BOATMAN
Eliza
b ca 1849
K. Stephen
Maria
b 1853
Measand
Jane
b 1856
Measand
With mother &
brother in 1901
Isabella
b 1858
Measand
Tom H.
b 1864
Measand
FARMER
Measand Beck
in 1901
Margaret J
b ca 1878
Ambleside
Alexandra M
b ca 1901
Ada Jane Maria b 1873
Janet Augusta Louisa b 1875 **
Tom Harrison Bousfield b 1876
Florence Winifred Hunter b 1878 *
Gladys Waistall L b 1880 *
William Theodore .B. b 1882 Kirby Stephen *, **
Lowther Lonsdale b 1883 *
Brunskill Hay B b 1884 *
Hugh Harvey H. b 1886 *
Arthur Hasell D. b 1887 *, **
Noble Bowstead H . b 1889 *, **
Selina Rose P. b1891 *, **
Albert Askington.D.S. b 1892**
Mabel Gertrude W. b 1893 **
Thomas Powsey b 1894
Elsie Violet C.F.M .b 1897 **
* AT SANDHILLS 1891
* * AT MEASAND COTTAGE IN 1901

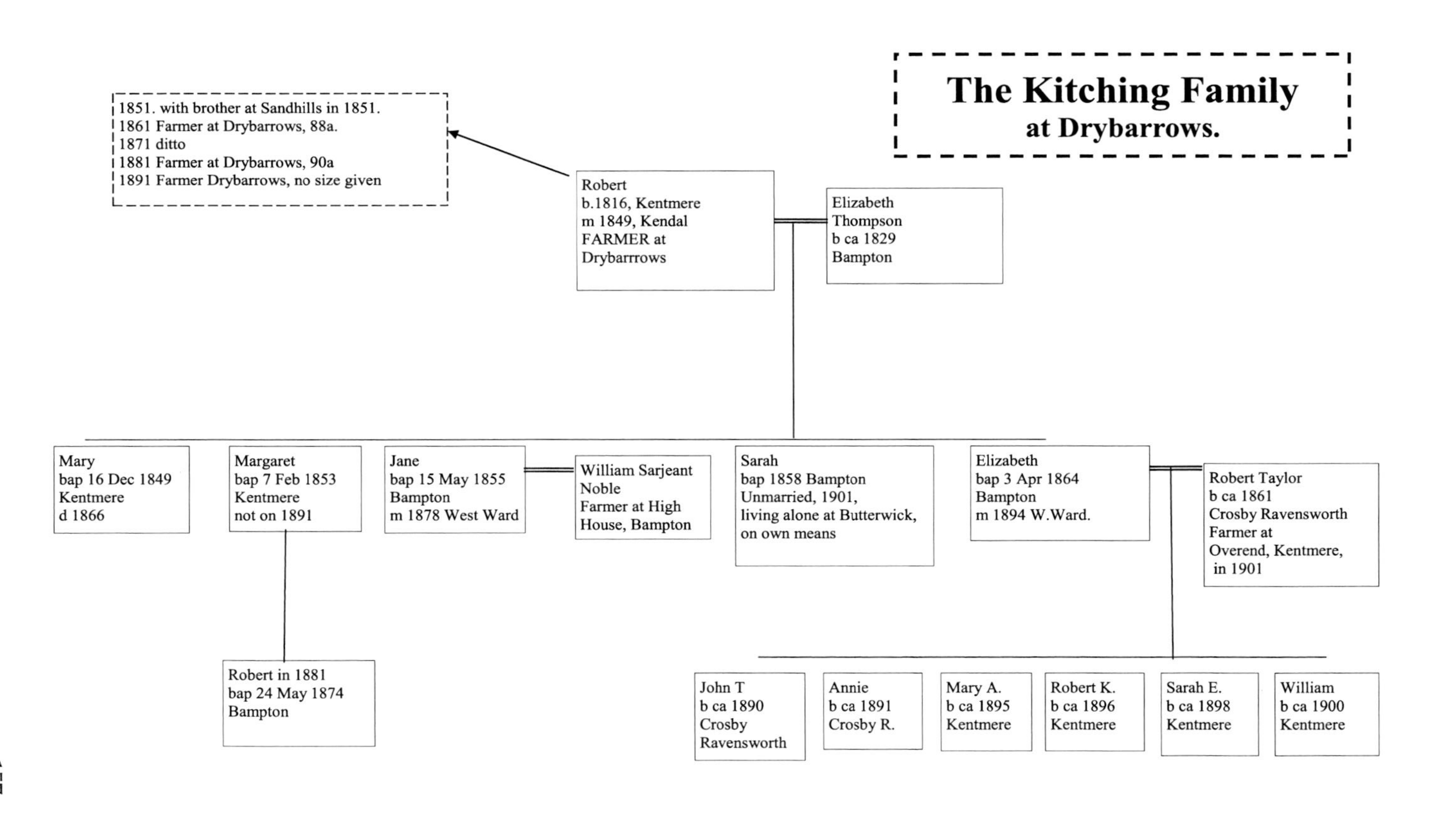

The Kitching Family
at Drybarrows.
1851. with brother at Sandhills in 1851.
1861 Farmer at Drybarrows, 88a.
1871 ditto
1881 Farmer at Drybarrows, 90a
1891 Farmer Drybarrows, no size given
Robert
b.1816, Kentmere
m 1849, Kendal
FARMER at
Drybarrrows
Elizabeth
Thompson
b ca 1829
Bampton
Mary
bap 16 Dec 1849
Kentmere
d 1866
Margaret
bap 7 Feb 1853
Kentmere
not on 1891
Jane
bap 15 May 1855
Bampton
m 1878 West Ward
William Sarjeant
Noble
Farmer at High
House, Bampton
Sarah
bap 1858 Bampton
Unmarried, 1901,
living alone at Butterwick,
on own means
Elizabeth
bap 3 Apr 1864
Bampton
m 1894 W.Ward.
Robert Taylor
b ca 1861
Crosby Ravensworth
Farmer at
Overend, Kentmere,
in 1901
Robert in 1881
bap 24 May 1874
Bampton
John T
b ca 1890
Crosby
Ravensworth
Annie
b ca 1891
Crosby R.
Mary A.
b ca 1895
Kentmere
Robert K.
b ca 1896
Kentmere
Sarah E.
b ca 1898
Kentmere
William
b ca 1900
Kentmere

were closely associated with the Holme family with several marriages occurring between the two families. Their Christian names mirrored those of the Holme family, namely John, Henrye, Heugh and William.

In 1686 a branch of the family had moved to the head of the valley when it is recorded that a son was born to 'William 'oth Greenhead', followed in 1694 by a daughter, Sarah. Sarah died in 1695, aged only a few months. Later that year another child was born and also named Sarah. It was common practice to give a child born later the same name but sadly she also died, aged only four months.

For many years after that the family lived in close association with the Holme family at Chapel Hill, occupying one of the cottages there. Jane, the first wife of William Jackson, died there in 1738. William died in 1760 and his second wife, Martha, in 1762. They were the last of the Jacksons recorded in Mardale.

THE GREEN FAMILY

John Green was born in Martindale, but may have been brought up by a family in Mardale. His ancestors had been in Martindale for at least four generations before him. He took up the tenancy of Sandhill in about 1749 when it is recorded that John Green of Measand married Margaret, daughter of John Miles of Rawside.

Their children John 1750, Mary 1752, Margaret 1754, Elizabeth 1756, Thomas 1759 and Joseph 1762 were all born at Sandhill.

John Green died in 1807 aged 89 at Butterwick Cragg, where he lived with his unmarried daughter Mary. He was described as 'late of Sandhill'.

Elizabeth, his daughter, married Richard Hindson in 1786. Known to all as Dick and Betty, in later life they lived in a cottage at Truss Gap in Swindale. They were both buried at Shap on the same day, 13th December 1838, aged 87 and 81. They had been found dead together. The inquest into their deaths was held at Appleby on 22nd December 1838.[4]

'An inquest was held before R.S. Stephenson, Esq, one of the Coroners for the County of Westmorland, on Wednesday at Swindale near Shap upon view of the bodies of Richard and Elizabeth Hindson,

man and wife, an aged couple who lived by themselves and were found, the Sunday morning previously lying on the floor of their cottage having only just arisen from bed, not having got themselves entirely dressed and preparations having been made for lighting the fire. It appeared that they had been only poorly off for some time back, and in a measure wanted the common necessaries of life.

Verdict – "died by the visitation of God"

Since the above inquisition it has been rumoured that the poor old people have not come by their death by fair means, but there is not sufficient ground to criminate anyone.'

Dick and Betty are said to haunt the road passing through the farmyard at Truss Gap.

Thomas, the second son of John and Margaret, married Agnes Pearson at Shap in 1790 and established a family at Sandhill. The third generation of Greens in Mardale was headed by Thomas and Agnes's son Joseph, or Jossie as he was known. Jossie was a famous character in the valley due to his willingness to sing at various events. It was said that *'the dalesman sings best when he has wetted his whistle'* and this was the way with Jossie Green of Naddle. When singing at the Dun Bull or after clipping at Thornthwaite he would be called upon for 'Tarry Woo', when he would sing the opening verse without accompaniment. The crowd would tease him, shouting *'thoos ower law, Jossie thoos ower law min, sup.'* So Jossie would *'knock his horn off'*(empty his glass or tankard). When his drink or *'horn'* was replenished he would start again. It may have taken several *'horns'* to get Jossie to the right pitch when there would be loud applause – *'theear, thoo's gitten it, Jossie, away wee it.'*

William Green 1853–1920, son of Jossie

Jossie, described as a shepherd, lived in Mardale, first at Sandhill, where he was born in 1812, and then Naddle until the late 1860s when he moved with his wife and son William to High Stead, Bretherdale and then to Sproatgyll at Orton, where he died in very sad circumstances in 1876.

Jossie's shepherds stick was passed down from eldest son to eldest son and is now in the prized possession of his great, great grandson, Michael W B Green.

While the Green name disappeared from Mardale with Jossie, the family ties remained through his daughter Hannah, who married George Greenhow, shepherd, of Mardale. They lived at first at Mosedale Cottage and then at the Dun Bull where George was the innkeeper for a time in the 1870s. Hannah died there on 15th November 1879 age 39, nineteen days after giving birth to her daughter Elizabeth. Shortly after her death George moved with his family to Naddle Farm, the childhood home of Hannah Green. George and Hannah's son, Tom George, stayed at Naddle and still occupied the farm in 1931.

THE WRIGHT FAMILY

Branches of this family lived in and around the Bampton/Mardale area for hundreds of years. Richard Wright of Drybarrows was involved in the establishment of Measand Grammar School.

The family are recorded in Measand from 1660. They probably occupied two of the very old farmsteads known as Seal Green and Waterside. Mary Wright died at Seal Green in 1673, Margaret in 1698 and William her husband in 1699. Another Margaret (nee Bowman) died at Seal Green in 1729, and was the last person recorded there. Matthew Wright was the son of Richard and Agnes Wright of Drybarrows, which at that time was part of the settlement of Measand. Matthew was born there along with three sisters. He married Sarah Castley at Bampton in 1729 and took over Colby Folds just up the lane from Seal Green in 1729.

Matthew and Sarah had two daughters, Agnes in 1730 and Ann in 1734. Sarah bore twins, Matthew and Mary, in 1737 but these children died within two months of their birth. Another girl, Sarah, was born in 1740. Matthew had no male heir.

Ann married the Reverend Richard Hebson, Curate of Mardale and Schoolmaster of Measand, in August 1765, two years after her mother Sarah died. Matthew Wright served as a churchwarden at St Patricks Church, Bampton in 1743 and 1755. He died at Colby in 1767, described in the burial register as *'ille Esculapides'* (Latin: a well known person)

At the beginning of the 19th century the records show an influx of new names. Movement was facilitated by new roads over easier routes. The Greenhows, Mawsons and Brunskills had arrived in the valley followed by many more names as people began to move father afield to make a living.

THE GREENHOW FAMILY

The family is first recorded in Mardale in 1766 when Thomas Greenhow the elder lived at Riggindale Farm. His wife Elizabeth died there in 1766. When he made his will there in 1779 he mentions his daughters Elizabeth, Agnes and Emma. Thomas and Elizabeth Greenhow's children were all born in Patterdale, but the girls were married in Bampton Parish in 1754 which suggests that the Greenhows were living somewhere in Mardale from that date. The residue of his estate was left to his son Thomas and grandson John who both succeeded him at Riggindale. The many descendants of Thomas and Agnes lived in Mardale for the next 130 years occupying Riggindale, Whelter, Goosemire, Brackenhowe and Naddle. They were very closely associated with the Holme family, being both tenants and employees. Two brothers, William and John, the eldest sons of John Greenhow and his second wife, Mary Winder, became assistant curates at Mardale Church. William died at the very early age of 25 in 1824.

One of the most notable members of the family was William Greenhow of Riggindale, known as 'The Shepherd'. His obituary in the Cumberland and Westmorland Herald described him as *'one of the best known and highly respected shepherds in the district. At one time he was head shepherd to the late Mr Hugh Holme of Chapel Hill.'*

Joseph Whiteside said of him:

'My favourite shepherd was Willie Greenhow of Riggindale, a very modest man with gentle features and manners. After a service he invariably pushed aside a vestry curtain and greeted me "Are ye gaily weel?" "Thank you Willie; I'm very fit; how are you." "I'se aw reet;

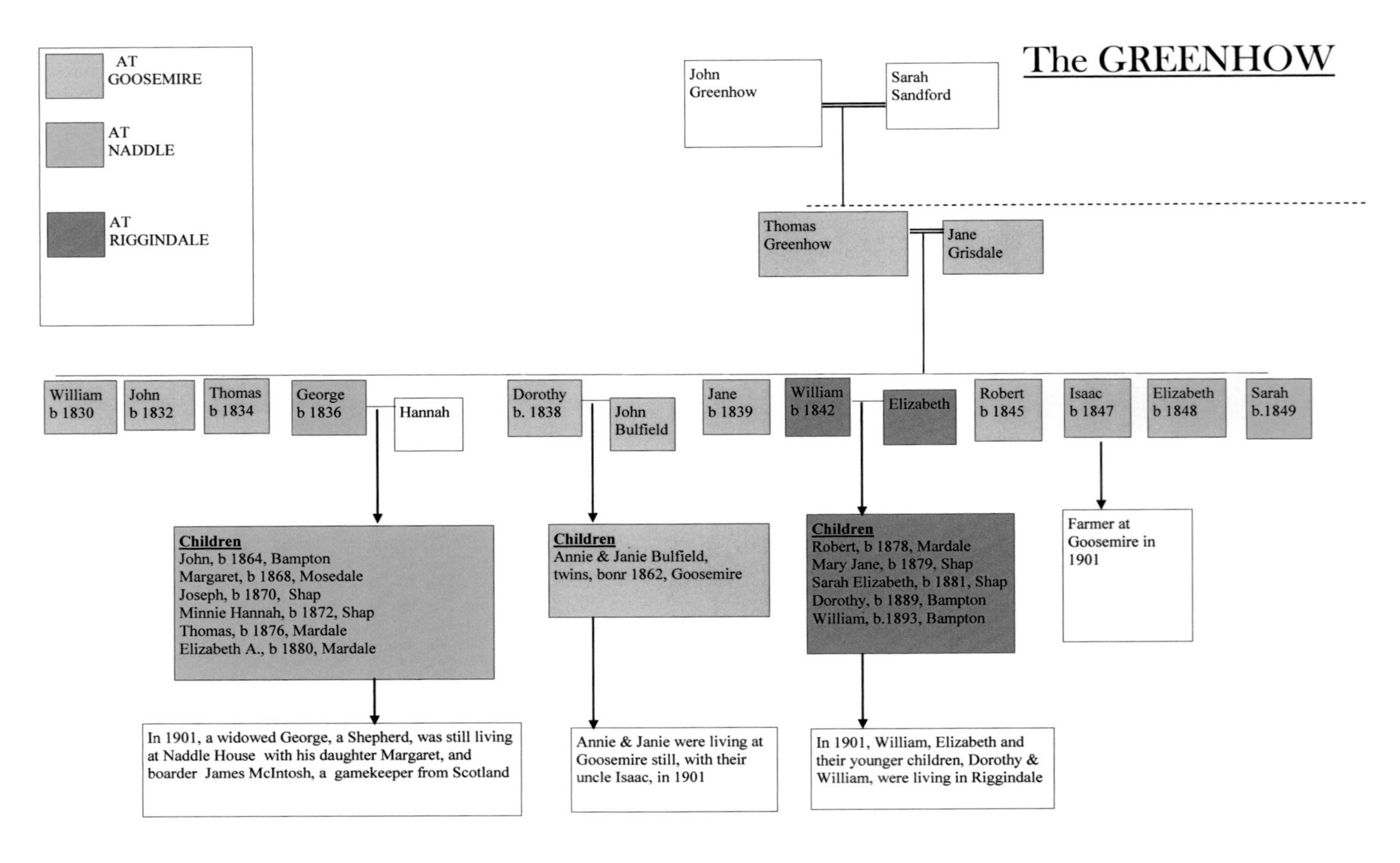

The GREENHOW
AT GOOSEMIRE
AT NADDLE
AT RIGGINDALE
John Greenhow
Sarah Sandford
Thomas Greenhow
Jane Grisdale
William b 1830
John b 1832
Thomas b 1834
George b 1836
Hannah
Dorothy b. 1838
John Bulfield
Jane b 1839
William b 1842
Elizabeth
Robert b 1845
Isaac b 1847
Elizabeth b 1848
Sarah b.1849
Children
John, b 1864, Bampton
Margaret, b 1868, Mosedale
Joseph, b 1870, Shap
Minnie Hannah, b 1872, Shap
Thomas, b 1876, Mardale
Elizabeth A., b 1880, Mardale
Children
Annie & Janie Bulfield, twins, bonr 1862, Goosemire
Children
Robert, b 1878, Mardale
Mary Jane, b 1879, Shap
Sarah Elizabeth, b 1881, Shap
Dorothy, b 1889, Bampton
William, b.1893, Bampton
Farmer at Goosemire in 1901
In 1901, a widowed George, a Shepherd, was still living at Naddle House with his daughter Margaret, and boarder James McIntosh, a gamekeeper from Scotland
Annie & Janie were living at Goosemire still, with their uncle Isaac, in 1901
In 1901, William, Elizabeth and their younger children, Dorothy & William, were living in Riggindale

Family

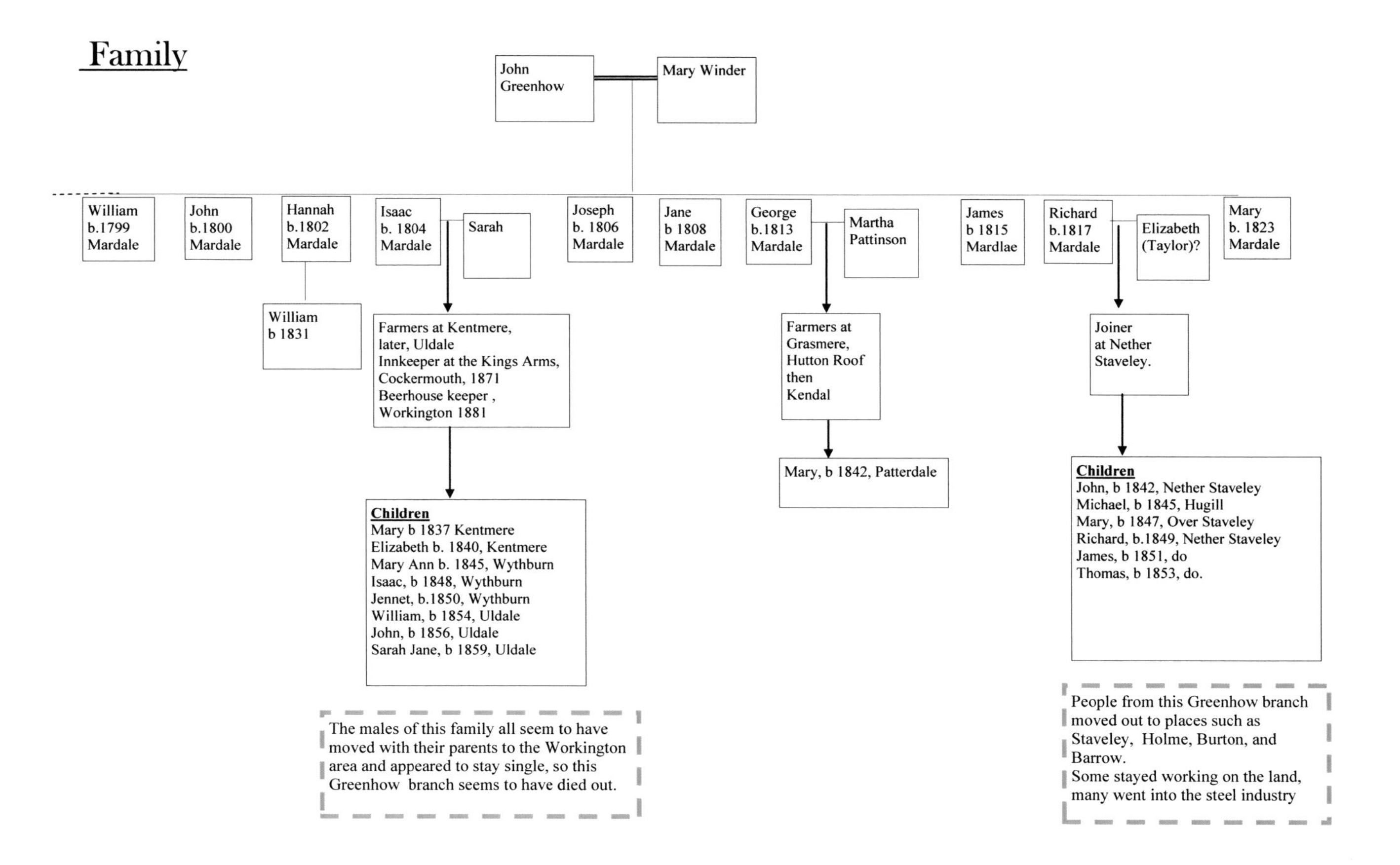

John Greenhow
Mary Winder
William b.1799 Mardale
John b.1800 Mardale
Hannah b.1802 Mardale
William b 1831
Isaac b. 1804 Mardale
Sarah
Farmers at Kentmere, later, Uldale Innkeeper at the Kings Arms, Cockermouth, 1871 Beerhouse keeper , Workington 1881
Children
Mary b 1837 Kentmere
Elizabeth b. 1840, Kentmere
Mary Ann b. 1845, Wythburn
Isaac, b 1848, Wythburn
Jennet, b.1850, Wythburn
William, b 1854, Uldale
John, b 1856, Uldale
Sarah Jane, b 1859, Uldale
The males of this family all seem to have moved with their parents to the Workington area and appeared to stay single, so this Greenhow branch seems to have died out.
Joseph b. 1806 Mardale
Jane b 1808 Mardale
George b.1813 Mardale
Martha Pattinson
Farmers at Grasmere, Hutton Roof then Kendal
Mary, b 1842, Patterdale
James b 1815 Mardlae
Richard b.1817 Mardale
Elizabeth (Taylor)?
Joiner at Nether Staveley.
Children
John, b 1842, Nether Staveley
Michael, b 1845, Hugill
Mary, b 1847, Over Staveley
Richard, b.1849, Nether Staveley
James, b 1851, do
Thomas, b 1853, do.
People from this Greenhow branch moved out to places such as Staveley, Holme, Burton, and Barrow.
Some stayed working on the land, many went into the steel industry
Mary b. 1823 Mardale

thank ye for t'lecture. Good neet." We were all such friends, members of a little family party.'(5)

A story related to Gwendolen Garston by Tommy Edmondson about Willie Greenhow inspired the following poem:

Hugh Holme – Shepherd

In Mardale churchyard, peacefully
five Greenhow brothers sleeping lie.
Four, side by side as once they lay
when children tired with their play.
But one the Shepherd lies apart,
beside his master who had his heart.
Shepherd and master, friend and friend
would not be parted at this life's end.

THE MOUNSEY FAMILY

The Mounseys were recorded in 1755 in Mardale when John and Elizabeth were living at Flakehow. They were members of a family who had lived in and around the vale of Bampton for many centuries. Another generation, namely Richard and Margaret, were at Mellbecks (Measand Beck Farm) in 1851.

Tom and Elizabeth Mounsey came to Whelter in 1892. They were one of the mainstays of the life of the valley in its latter days, always mentioned in reports of any of the functions, including concerts, tea parties, and suppers.

THE MAWSON AND DEWHIRST FAMILIES

The Mawson family first appear in Mardale in 1841 when Aaron was the tenant at Goosemire. It is not certain where he came from but it is probable that the Aaron Mawson who was born at Irton in Cumberland was the same person. He was followed at Goosemire by his son, also named Aaron. His other son, George, farmed at Grove Brae for some time before moving to Orton, where his descendants still live.

Aaron the second never married and was looked after by his sister Agnes. Agnes had a daughter, Ann, who married Robinson Dewhurst, member of a Shap family. Robinson took over Goosemire on Aaron's retirement but moved the whole family to Clifton around 1875. Aaron died at Clifton in 1884.

Robinson and Ann, with their children, moved away from Cumbria to Hinkley, Warwickshire very shortly after Aaron's death, where they farmed at Shelford House. Agnes died there, far away from her Mardale home, in 1888.

THE EDMONDSON FAMILY

The Edmondson family came to Flakehow in 1890. Thomas and his wife Isabella came from Barton where Thomas had been born in 1856. Their children Mary, Ada, Annie, Thomas and Hannah were born at Barton and Maggie and John George were born at Flakehow.

The Edmondsons figured largely in the life of the

The children of Maggie (nee Edmondson) and Jack Lancaster
Left to right , Alec, Marion, Raymond, Maggie and Jack

community, Thomas serving as a church warden for many years. He was the source of many of the stories of Mardale gathered by Gwendoline Garston. He had a wealth of them which he told over and over again.

Joseph Whiteside recalls:

'Another crony, a good fellow of a different type was Tom Edmonson of Flake How. Honest laughter is a gift of the gods. He would beckon me to him in sundry places such as Bampton or Penrith "Cum her a minnut; I'v gitten yan for y"'[5]

Whiteside continued:

'The incident is not so much as the manner of its telling, and it's a poor story if the narrator himself doen't enjoy it. Tom was a stoutish lad with a round jovial face; and he bubbled with mischievous spirit while he gripped his rotundity with both hands, quivering like a tumultuous jelly shaken by internal convulsions as he leant against a wall for support.'

This sense of humour was inherited by his son Tom who was an equal to his father in the telling of stories and was imbued with the same mischievous spirit as his father.

In the early twentieth century the occupants of the valley became unsettled by the plans to build a damn. The Kitchings, Edmondsons and Greenhows remained from the old days. Bob Daffurn stayed at the Dun Bull until 1933. He left the running of the hotel in the hands of his daughter Lucy and her husband Maurice Bell. Other families who came in the latter days did not stay for long. They included the Watsons, Hudsons, Hindsons and Newtons.

The Edmondson family at Flakehow

Back left, Tom,
back right, John
Left to right, Polly, Annie, Hannah, Maggie, Ada
In front,
Thomas P Edmondson and his wife, Sarah

Chapter 10

Days of Exploration and Adventure

Baily family sketch by G H J Baily

For at least two families, Mardale was a favourite holiday destination. The Baily family first visited in 1914 and the Hay family in 1916. Both families were in the valley at the same period, and were known to one another.

In 1912 the Reverend George Baily was appointed vicar of Burneside to the north of Kendal, the following year he took his wife Mary (who was in the early stages of her sixth pregnancy) and his sister Belle on a weeks' walking tour in the Lakes. They had left their five children in the care of their nanny, servants, Aunt Maud Garston, Mrs Baily's elder sister, and her daughter Gwendolen. On the last day, their route took them from Patterdale over Kidsty Pike and down into the valley of Mardale where they were to stay the night at the Dun Bull Hotel. Before setting out for home over Gatescarth Pass the following morning, Mrs Baily noticed that the two farm cottages attached to the Dun Bull Hotel, Goosemire and Grove Brae, were vacant. 'This', she said, 'is where we're bringing the children for a holiday' and in 1914, the whole family came to Mardale for the first time. For fifteen years, until 1929 when they had to leave, they came to stay at every conceivable opportunity.

When the family came to Mardale they all came, with the children's nanny and maids, and household pets. Most of the family came by train to Shap, from where they were conveyed in the Dun Bull carriage. Some of the party began what was to become a common practice of cycling up Long Sleddale,

Reverend George and Mary Baily

leaving their bicycles at Sadgill, and walking over Gatescarth Pass. The account of this visit is to be found in the only edition of the 'Mardale Mercury' dated Wednesday 14th August 1914, with Daddy Baily as Editor. This is a single broadsheet paper divided into columns, but not completely filled. He reports on the 'Arrival of the Baily Family' thus:

'They came – They came – They came in crowds. There were so many of them that they nearly burst the Dale and let the Lake out. Their luggage was a high as Kidsty Pike. There was Daddy and Mammy and Dick and Dulcie and Stephen and Helena and Roger and Thomas E. H. Baily Esq. and Rufus and Smoke with a bag full of smoked mice and Jet with his toothbrush and Ninny and Annie and Rachel and Nelly and the luggage and they came to Grove Brae and Goosemire and climbed some fells.'

The above account is scattered with charming sketches. Thomas E H Baily aged eight months, was depicted as a baby holding a dummy, as an adult he was a long serving vicar of Shap. The cats are shown carrying a bag and toothbrush. Four ladies in the group are shown riding bicycles and the luggage is piled high on a cart with some of it falling off.

Helena, who later became a school teacher at Penrith Grammar School, recalled that her first really conscious recollection was on the 5th August 1914 when her father went out to meet the postman, Harry Pearson, who had come out from Shap on his bicycle and brought the newspapers. She remembered the spot beside a little beck below Hopgill, where her father opened the newspaper and read that the war had been declared.

The Baily children at Goosemire 1927
L to R: Roger, Dick, John, Dulcie, Helena, Stephen and Tom

The Bailys were a much extended family and for that first year they took over both Grove Brae and Goosemire. The children were housed at Goosemire in the care of nanny and the maids and the adults mostly at Grove Brae. The family consisted of the mother and father and six children, four boys and two girls. Another brother was born two years later. The party often included Mrs Baily's older sister Aunt Maud, a widow who lived near Burneside, and her grown up daughter Gwendolen Garston who was in the Land Army. Gwendolen worked for a short time at Crosby Ravensworth and then for family reasons had to live at home, but she was never far away from Mardale. She used to go over for lambing, clipping, and hay time; she was a hard worker and much in demand by the local farmers who often summoned her to work by post card.

The family had the two cottages for a year and then Harry Walker went to live at Grove Brae as farm man for the Dun Bull, so the Bailys were left with Goosemire, which they rented for ten pounds a year. They were able to rent Goosemire so long as the shepherd was a single man, but if a married man had been engaged he would have wanted the cottage. When

Goosemire was not available for them, the Bailys were able to rent Riggindale on the same terms, which was the cottage for the farm man at Chapel Hill. As the cottage was rented for a year, the children came every Easter and summer holiday, sometimes at Whitsuntide if they could, and when the brothers were older they would come over in the winter. Mrs Baily was a generous person so no matter who arrived she always managed to fit them in somewhere.

During the fifteen years when they holidayed in the dale, the family produced their own home-made newspapers, bearing the titles, 'The Goosemire Guardian' or the 'The Riggindale Record', according to which house they were renting at the time. Each member of the family and any guests were invited to picture a particular theme, or write poems and stories. These were judged and awarded marks, and then all the efforts were hand-sewn into little books the size of an exercise book. At the end of the holidays all the votes were counted and Aunt Maud gave a prize of half-a-crown to the winner, a tidy addition to pocket money. The covers are wonderful, as are Dulcie's paintings of Mardale flowers, and her father's charming pen and ink sketches. Artwork by Helena shows how her skill developed. Gwendolen Garston's contributions took the form of detailed diary entries describing their activities and she occasionally included snippets of Mardale history which she had gleaned from the locals. In all, these provide a wonderful contemporary record of the dale as it was in the 1920s. In wet summers the family produced a newspaper every week but if the weather was good, fewer were produced.

During the First World War, Mr Baily served as a chaplain with the army and as part of their war effort, the family gathered sphagnum moss when they were on holiday. Once a week they took two large sacks and went up Riggindale, because that was the best place, into a large area of boggy ground where they gathered the bright green, red and yellow sphagnum moss. It was carried back to Goosemire where it was spread on newspapers in the wash house to dry. On a picking afternoon, the women in the family sat round and picked all the bits of grass and stick out of the moss. It was bagged up and sent into Penrith where it was used as absorbent dressings in the two army hospitals there. Helena recalled that as children they often used sphagnum moss as a dressing when they cut a toe running about bare foot.

The family had old clothes known as the Mardale clothes, which were kept in a large trunk. Every holiday time these were pulled out of the trunk and aired. Helena tells us that:

'Tom was rather a loner. Whilst the rest of us ran about in any old clothes with bare legs and often bare feet, Tom always solemnly wore a collar and tie, a neat jacket and knee length socks and shoes.'

Those who knew Tom in later life when he was vicar of Shap will vouch for his smart way of dressing – normally in a suit, sometimes tweed with plus-fours if the occasion merited, always with a brightly coloured silk handkerchief in his breast pocket. He did not wear a 'dog-collar', preferring a white bow tie and wing collar, and on rare occasions a standard collar and tie. His hat was always a flat cap but he would wear overalls when tinkering with his beloved motor cycle.

The family possessed 'bathing dresses', an assorted collection of blue cotton, shapeless, unisex garments which were worn when the family swam in the lake at Guerness Bay.

Swimming at Guerness – family sketch

The shore sloped out gently here and there was a sandy bottom, safe for paddlers and swimmers alike. They also swam beneath some of the waterfalls in the mountain becks. Helena remembered how they plunged into the pool which took some courage because it was so icy, and then they would sit under the waterfall, get out again, be rubbed down, and given a ginger biscuit which was supposed to warm you up.

When they were staying in Riggindale, Dick once dammed the Randale beck to create a harbour for his model battleships which were from plans in 'Jane's Fighting Ships'. Higher up the stream was a little clapper bridge and higher still a bathing pool with a waterfall. The children went all over the place, as children will, they roamed the fells and had picnics.

'A large basket would be packed with a loaf or two of bread, some bully beef, a pat of butter, some cheese and a packet of Mapletons Fruitavian Cake – a firm mixture of dried fruit, dried banana and nuts which was cut up into small squares about the size of your thumbnail, and the delicious Wimco dried bananas – known to the children as 'dead men's fingers' which rather upset Mother.'

They explored and got to know every inch of the valley though their holidays were not all play and adventure. In the morning there were jobs to do at Goosemire. Whoever was doing the cooking had to get up early and take the breakfast porridge out of the hay-box where it had quietly cooked all night. Then somebody had to go and fetch the water, because the Goosemire water supply was about fifty yards away, on the 'intak' field called the Girsings, where a water pipe brought the water off the fellside into a butt. The farm was called Goosemire because round the cottage was very boggy ground, used to graze geese.

After a day spent out of doors the family gathered for high tea, a filling meal with only two alternatives, both from the hay-box. The hay-box was an old tuck box thickly lined with hay, two cushions of hay were placed on top and the lid closed. Helena recalled:

'Cousin Gwendolen would prepare the evening meal, either a stew or a mysterious dish called Savoury Barley. This was boiled up in a large iron pan and then put quickly into its nest in the hay-box; there

it simmered happily all day ready for the evening. Savoury barley was a type of pilau mixture using barley instead of rice cooked in a meat stock with onions, tomatoes and raisins plus any meat left-overs, the whole served with grated cheese.' She also recalled the legendary jelly: *'sometimes plain and sometimes with a banana, the curious thing was that Cousin Gwendolen never made more than one pint, no matter how many of us there were; it was my job to give everyone a fair share, this could be tricky with an odd number of people and resulted in only about two spoonfuls each. A disgusting way of eating jelly, frowned upon by the adults if they noticed, was to swill a spoonful round your mouth and then decant it back into the spoon, so that when you put it back in your mouth you virtually had two spoonfuls from the original one.'*

On one occasion Dick and Stephen had gone to stay at Goosemire by themselves when they were in their late teens, and decided to make themselves a rice pudding in the hay-box. Not knowing the nature of rice, they filled the pan to the brim and added some water. When they returned in the evening the hay-box lid had been pushed open by a solid column of rice rising from the pan!

After tea they settled to card games such as Beggar My Neighbour, Old Maid and County Cards – a game based on towns in various counties with rules similar to Happy Families – paper games such as Consequences, Heads, Bodies and Legs, or reading. Aunt Maud kept them supplied with the latest John Buchan or Stanley Weyman, there were also volumes of American annuals and Boy's Own paper, the girls preferring this to Girl's Own. In the background Mr Barham's gramophone would be playing, and games had to be interrupted in order to wind up the gramophone or change the needle.

The nearest picnic place was up Hopgill beck, where there was a wealth of rare ferns; and they explored, the boys trying to find some reputed caves. In Guerness wood, the family explored the remains of the old copper mine, the boys venturing some way into the mine shafts. Another expedition was to Bowderthwaite, where there was a beautiful bathing pool under the bridge and a lovely waterfall. Sometimes the family would disperse and lie about among the rough grass very quietly, because they might see a lizard or a grasshopper, a woolly bear caterpillar or a big black beetle. We are told that somewhere up in Mardale are two boot button eyes which some archaeologist may find one day. Little Tom had a soft toy named Brown Doggie; and one day he came home without his favourite toy, so everyone went back and searched to no avail. Tom could only be comforted by being told *'Well, Brown Doggie's lucky. He's in Mardale all the year round. He doesn't have to go back to beastly Sunderland.'*

In Riggindale there was some boggy ground where the family looked for flowers - the first Grass of Parnassus of the summer, sundew and ranunculus - marsh marigold and globe flower, the Alpine catchfly, the large violet butterwort and milkwort. These discoveries gave the greatest pleasure. High on Harter Fell they found roseroot sedum and they found it again on Castle Crag. Up the Randale beck there were dragonflies - everywhere they went there was something really special to discover. Also in Riggindale, close to Bowderthwaite, there was a little hillock with a steep rock slide about ten or twelve feet long, ideal for sliding down in iron soled clogs and smoothed by generations of children doing the same. It should still be possible to locate this rock as it will be above the lakeshore.

Mrs Baily was a native of Hampshire and wrote her memories for the newspaper of her old home at Wickham. These articles are a delight to read. She became deeply involved with Mardale and its people, often playing the organ at the church and arranging flowers.

Mr Barham was described by Helena as *'the dearest, kindest, most saintly old man who was real parish priest to the dale and to any visitors who came.'* He was a bachelor and lived in the enormous Victorian vicarage, all by himself, without a housekeeper. As soon as the Baily family arrived, either at Goosemire or Riggindale, he would call straight away, taking over one of his gramophones for their pleasure, with the most amazing collection of records - good classical, light classical, together with wartime songs, soldier's songs and popular songs including 'K-K-K-Katy'. He would call on the family once a week and was very fond of Mrs Baily and her sister, and loved talking to them. On one occasion whilst he was chatting with them, Mr Baily came into the room and joined in the conversation. Mr Barham was rather put out by this interruption and promptly pulled the newspaper out of his raincoat pocket, saying to Mr Baily 'Would you like to look at the paper?'

Whilst the family spent their long holidays in Mardale, their father did not ignore the needs of his parishioners in Burneside and on several occasions he walked over Gatescarth and through Long Sleddale to Burneside to take the necessary services, returning the same day. On one occasion he returned with a table that would be useful at Goosemire strapped to his back. He had unscrewed the legs and tied them together separately to make his burden less awkward.

The family also enjoyed picnics down by the lake. Sometimes they would have the use of the Dun Bull boat and go down to Guerness Bay which was about a half-mile walk from Goosemire. They always built a fire on the beach, and Mr Baily would carry down a large iron pot of potatoes, which they boiled up on the fire, a great treat to eat on a wet day huddled under their mackintoshes with the rain pouring down.

George Baily wrote this little ditty:

'There is a broad bay down in Guerness
Where our family revel in bareness
And Mother brings soap
In the praiseworthy hope
Of reducing their sunburn to fairness!'

In the early 1920s the Bailys moved to Christ Church, Penrith, and Helena attended Penrith Grammar School where she was later to become a teacher. Later in that decade they moved to Sunderland. The family disliked being so far away from Westmorland, and their visits to Mardale were anticipated with even more excitement. Helena recalled in her notes on the holidays:

'After we went to Sunderland, the transport of the cats was quite a problem, as they were supposed to travel in the guard's van with a

ticket. We always filled a whole compartment ourselves, stuffed with hand luggage, and the cat baskets secreted under the seats. They meowed a good deal, but miraculously, when the ticket collector came round, they always lapsed into silence. They always sensed when we were packing up to go home at the end of the holiday and managed to disappear up the fell to be caught with a great deal of trouble. The only female cat who went to Mardale with us was pure white called Snowball'; kittens were rather a problem, so one year she was donated to Chapel Hill and happily produced white and mixed descendents who became well known throughout the dale.'

The Goosemire Guardian of April 1927 contains accounts of the kind of journey each member of the family would choose from Sunderland to Mardale. One chose to travel by train, whilst another would walk the Roman Wall then take a train from Carlisle to Penrith and walk to Mardale via Askham.

The Reverend Baily was good at making things, and he decided to build a punt. The family newspapers record the building of this punt which they intended to sail on the river. They went all the way down to Guerness Bay carrying the punt on a wheelbarrow which Mr Baily had constructed for the job of gathering kindling, known as 'sticking'. Just before the lake there was a calm bit of the river called Flybeck Dub, and so the

The punt

punt was named the *'Wild Goose'* and duly launched. Two of the boys got in, sat down and then Mr Baily stepped in wearing his Oxford punting hat, with his punt pole made from a stick off the fellside. Their elderly aunt, who was the guest of honour, climbed in with her blue cloak and her straw hat, and the punt promptly foundered with all hands!

Helena's first climb was up Kidsty Pike in 1917 when she was seven. For years she kept her alpenstock, a hazel stick with her name and the date on it. They would go roaming up Dudderwick where they discovered owls in a barn, and onto Harter Fell, from there to explore round Small Water, then to Blea Water.

Helena recalled:

'Jobs done, we were ready for off. The weather was no problem. Wet or fine we put on our stout boots or shoes and macs if necessary and a good scarf or hat as the wind could be cold on the tops and earache could be agonising. As we got older, Dulcie and I found that the fashionable hairstyle of 'ear-phones' was a great protection. Only if the rain was absolutely pelting down, did we stay at home. Just very occasionally we had a little snow in the Easter holidays, and on one occasion Aunt B (Kathleen O'Brien – a childhood friend of Cousin Gwendolen) organised ice cream; a custard mixture packed into a tin and then put into a bucket packed with a mixture of snow and salt and left outside. It was an experiment rather than a luxury, with a flaky but quite edible texture.'

Every summer the family enjoyed one great expedition. One year they had an expedition up the Corpse Road, over the fell, and down into Swindale where Mrs Cragg of Truss Gap gave them a splendid egg tea at a cost of ninepence for the children and a shilling for the grown ups, with the brothers still counted as children despite being six foot tall!

The Hay family also took holidays in the valley at the same time as the Bailys.

The Hay family consisted of the father, mother and two sons, David and Michael. Thomas Hay was a headmaster and mathematician, fellow of the Royal Geological Society, and keen amateur archaeologist. His wife, who was described as tempestuous, artistic and quite unpredictable, swept into Mardale but never really became part of it. David Hay wrote of his holiday memories in the book 'Mardale, the drowned village' published by Friends of the Lake District in 1976.[1] Mrs Hay kept a diary, and this contains some references to the Bailys.

The two families are recorded as taking part in a joint activity on 30th June 1922 when an excavation was carried out on Castle Crag, by Professor W.G. Collingwood, Reverend Baily, Miss Hodgson, Miss Garston, and Thomas Hay with his son David. The Baily archive dated 9th September 1922 includes a detailed drawing of the fort with some humorous comments:

'The whole day with minute-intervals for meals was spent in digging a trench from the nearest outcrop of rock to the centre of the ridge. The excavators were satisfied; i) that the hole they had made was great, ii) that the heap they had made was greater, iii) that the existence of an earthwork on the brow of the cliff was proved. The fort by this discovery is shewn to be elliptical in plan. Valuable but scanty finds were made of charcoal at a depth of 15 inches from the surface of the newly discovered earthwork. The exploratory trench was filled in on Friday. The genius of the digger-in-chief as a landscape gardener was taxed to the uttermost by the heap of soil remaining after the hole had been filled up.'

During the 1920s the Baily family found they had a war on their hands. Manchester Corporation was going to drown their beloved lake and beautiful valley and they were dismayed to find that nobody was doing anything about it. Nobody, that is, except the militant Bailys! There is a splendid entry in Gwendolyn's diary *'The children had a happy day pulling up the Manchester surveyor's marking posts-Bless them.'* These were wooden posts marking the 100 foot level. The children just went round, pulled the posts out of the ground and threw them away. The work would then be done again with similar results, so that in the end the surveyors had to do their work when the Bailys were not there. Mrs Baily, a very mild person normally, met one of the young engineers and said to him *'Young man, what do you think you're doing?'* He replied *'Just doing my job'*, and she said *'Well young man, you had better give up this job and get another one.'*

Mr Isaac Hinchcliffe, a Manchester city councillor, wrote a

book called 'A Backwater in Lakeland'[2] The family considered Mr Hinchcliffe to be the enemy because the council were about to destroy the valley. Helena recalled how, as a child of about thirteen, she was walking down the road when she met Mr Hinchcliffe who was dispensing autographed copies of his book. He presented her with a copy. She was too polite and shy to say anything, so just thanked him meekly and took it home. The family were very united - and that day they were united against her, for bringing the enemy's book home.

In 1929 the family had their last holiday in Mardale as Manchester Corporation wanted Goosemire to house two of their engineers and could offer a higher rent. Despite the sadness at leaving their beloved holiday home, the family were all growing up and leaving home. Dick was in the army and stationed in India, Dulcie had finished at Art School in Sunderland, and was about to become engaged. The engagement was later broken off and Dulcie went out to Canada with Kathleen O'Brien, a missionary, in British Columbia. Dulcie loved the place and got a job at a residential school for native Canadian children, and where she met her future husband, who was working out there too. Stephen was at Oxford, Helena was about to start her studies at Bristol University and Roger, Tom and John were still at school.

The following year they had an exchange holiday in their old vicarage at Burneside. By chance they heard that the living at Patterdale was vacant. Mr Baily contacted the patrons and the bishop and he and his wife went over to look at the Rectory and the parish in general. Having no car they took the train to Penrith and the bus to Patterdale in great secrecy. When they arrived at the Rectory, they found to their horror that the children and their aunt were already there, having managed to get into the Rectory through an unlatched window and had chosen their bedrooms!

How had they managed this feat? Aunt Maud had hired a bus and, as soon as the parents had departed to the station, the bus appeared and they drove over Kirkstone Pass to Patterdale. The decision was made to abandon Sunderland and they were settled at Patterdale in time for Christmas. Someone said to

Brait Wilson, the huntsman for the Ullswater Foxhounds *'You'll know Mr Baily won't you'*, and he said *'Aye, Mr Baily, he's a grand preacher, but he's got a gey untidy lot o' children.'*

Mardale was an ideal place for relaxation, with freedom to explore. Towards the end of her life, Helena described Mardale as she remembered it:

'Looking back now I like to think how enormously, enormously blessed we as children were to have the experience of loving the most beautiful, beautiful valley God ever created.'

Front cover of the Goosemire Guardian

Chapter 11

Artists, Writers and Poets

Artists

The picturesque qualities of Mardale have attracted many artists over the years, and there is a considerable number of steel etchings of scenes around the valley. The best known are those of Mardale Green in 1820 which show the tower on Wood Howe, Measand falls by J. B. Pyne, and High Street showing horses racing on the summit by T Allam and J W Lowry. Other prints depict the tarns above Haweswater, and a packhorse train traversing Gatescarth Pass.

There is a steel engraving dated 1773 entitled 'A view of Haweswater a lake near Banton in Westmorland' by Chatalen and Miller after a painting by Wllm. Neers. This was commissioned by James Lowther and shows a view from the dale head looking down the lake; in the foreground is a party of people in a punt. The topographical features are not readily identified; two buildings are to be seen on the western side of the lake and Guerness Nib on the eastern shore. This work is displayed at Wordsworth House in Cockermouth.

One of the most notable local artists, Jacob Thompson, was born at Penrith in 1806. He was familiar with Mardale and set several of his romantic oil paintings in the valley, one 'Drawing the net on Haweswater' painted in 1867 was obviously executed at the request of his patron, the Earl of Lonsdale, since it depicts the Earl with guests seated around a boat. Another painting depicting a boat on the lake is 'Holiday on Hawes-Water' also known as 'Pleasure Party on Hawes-Water'.

Two other works intended for viewing as a pair are 'The Height of Ambition' and 'The Downfall of Pride', the first showing a group of children drawing a makeshift sled with four occupants up a mountainside; the second shows the overturned sled with the occupants upon the ground and others attempting to right it. These two paintings are now in the possession of Penrith Museum. Both show the view from above Measand and include the portraits of Hugh Parker Holme, the last King of Mardale, and his brother; they portray a moral story, this trait being attributed to Thompson's Quaker roots. When in Mardale, Mr Thompson stayed at Measand Beck Hall as the guest of Mr Bland. The way in which he depicted the landscape, and especially the sky, were so accurate that when a local shepherd, saw the painting 'Holiday on Haweswater', he read the sky, drift of smoke and mist in the painting and confirmed them to be accurate 'signs of fine weather'.

Thompson also painted the two murals that frame the east window of St Andrew's Church in Penrith. He ended his days at the Hermitage in Hackthorpe and died in 1879. He is buried in Lowther churchyard. 'Life, the biography of Jacob Thompson' by Llewellyn Jewitt was privately published in 1882 and gives a fuller account of Thompson's activities.

Jacob Thompson

A watercolour of Haweswater in 1881, by William Taylor Longmire, shows Measand looking towards the dale head. Thomas Bland, the talented artist and sculptor from Reagill, made four pen and ink sketches of Mardale Chapel, Chapel Hill and the lake which date from about 1845.

A friend and distant relative of Jacob Thompson was Samuel Lucas, senior, who was a keen watercolour painter, and Thompson introduced him to Haweswater, taking him to stay at Measand Beck Hall. Lucas's children would sometimes come with him and over the years they developed a love of the area. The son, Samuel Lucas, junior, became a proficient artist and several of his works of Haweswater and Mardale still survive in private collections. His sisters Anne and Matilda were also artists and ceramic painters and were also the authors of 'Two Englishwomen in Rome'. They eventually gave up their high life in Rome and at the turn of the twentieth century and came to live at Stanegarth above Bampton.

They were real characters: Anne was short and stout, gruff in manner and smoked a clay pipe, whilst Matilda was tall, dignified and gracious with a good sense of humour. They were very old fashioned in their dress and lived simply without luxuries. They kept horses and pigs and were keen gardeners. They had a wide circle of influential friends including Canon Hardwicke Rawnsley and his wife, the artist Sir Lawrence Alma-Tadema, and Hugh Walpole who based the house Stone Ends in his novel 'Judith Paris' on Stanegarth. A watercolour painting of Haweswater by Matilda Lucas was sold at auction in August 2010, mainly executed in a series of washes, showing a small reed fringed promontory with the lake and fells behind.

Alfred Heaton Cooper made some delightful paintings of the valley during his visit to Measand in 1925. The artist wrote of a visit to Measand in the book 'The English Lakes':[1]

'I don't know whether it was the exceptional beauty of those still autumn days or the knowledge that, in a few years time, this valley would be under water, that gave our stay at Measand a poignancy that can still affect me over forty years later.' He spoke affectionately of Measand Falls *'that come down in two tiers with several cascades between steep rocky islands open to the sun and sky.'*

Bampton church has a watercolour dating from the mid 19th century of Mardale church in the snow, painted by Jabez Lowthian, a native of Renwick near Penrith. Caroline Crompton, who painted scenes in Mardale in the first quarter of the twentieth century, was the daughter of Reverend William Crompton, the vicar of Shap, and was a prolific watercolour artist and a member of the Lakes Artists Society. St. Michael's Church, Shap owns some of her works including one of Mardale Church. Other views of the Mardale area that she painted include: 'First snow on Haweswater fells' (1921), 'A glimpse of Haweswater' (1924), 'A June morning, Haweswater' (1925), 'A stormy day on Haweswater' (1925), 'Haweswater and Harter Fell' (1927), 'Haweswater' (1936) 'Haweswater and Harter Fell' (again in

1936), 'Haweswater and Naddle' (1936). Unfortunately the whereabouts of these paintings is not known; details of the titles and exhibition dates are courtesy of the Lakes Artists Society.

An oil painting entitled 'Old Mill near Haweswater' by William James Blacklock, dated 1854, shows a quaint watermill with an overshot wheel amongst woodland. The Baily family created paintings and drawings of Mardale during their holidays which provide a charming and amusing record of their activities. Helena Baily continued to paint and teach art as an adult and left some lovely watercolour views of Mardale to her family and friends.

Alfred Wainwright did many meticulous pen and ink drawings of Haweswater and its fells. In his BBC interview with Eric Robson for 'Wainwright on Lakeland's Far Eastern Fells' (1985) he describes his first visit in the 1930s when he found *"Mardale – a bright jewel in a dark crown"*. Down in the valley he saw wild roses in the hedgerows, shady trees and heard birdsong, but there was no sign of life. He found the homes were deserted and abandoned. Never, he said, had he ever seen a more beautiful picture, nor a sadder one.

In 1985 he said *'This in my opinion is the finest valley head in the Lake District, not so grand perhaps as Wasdale and possibly Langdale; but so beautifully arranged, symmetrically arranged, completely encircling the floor of the valley. The only escape really is along the valley which is flooded; but this gives it a greater sense of isolation.'*

Jonathan Otley, in his book 'English Lakes', includes a panoramic sketch of Haweswater identifying the various features and in 'Highways and Byways in the Lake District' by A G Bradley there is an illustration of Haweswater by Joseph Pennel. Today there are many other artists and photographers, professional and amateur, who are inspired by the beauty and scenery of the valley.

Writers

Haweswater has always been the most remote and least visited of the Lakes. The lake is omitted from Speeds map of Westmorland of 1676, and it was not included in the plans of the Lakes published by Crosthwaite in 1785 and Clarke in 1787. One of the earliest guides to the Lakes was written by Jonathan Otley[2] and published in 1850. He devotes a page to Hawes Water and describes it as follows:

'Lying beyond the usual circuit of the lakes, and at a distance from the great roads and places of entertainment, Hawes Water is often omitted. But tourists, who can contrive to visit it without hurry or fatigue, will find it a sweet retired spot.'

In a section on routes around the Lakes he gives details for an outing on horseback or on foot to Haweswater from Kendal through Longsleddale or Kentmere, describing the route from Kentmere over Nan Bield Pass as *'still more difficult'*, though weary travellers would find the Dun Bull at Mardale Green *'no alarming or unwelcome object.'* He describes the route to Haweswater from Bampton as *'four miles of indifferent carriage road.'*

David Holt, writing in 1856,[3] describes a three day ramble in the Lake District and a walk along the north western shore of Haweswater to the valley head where he found the scenery *'strikingly grand and calculated to inspire unusually solemn feelings.'* Over the years many other guide books have been published, and many of these include descriptions of Mardale and Haweswater.

Other writers and novelists also found inspiration in Mardale; Anne Ward Radcliffe's 'Journey' made in 1768 includes a description of her visit to Mardale, and Arthur Mees 'Lake Counties' (1937) also describes the valley, noting its destruction. The Lake Counties by W G Collingwood contains descriptions of Haweswater and Mardale together with several nice illustrations by A. Reginald Smith. The iconic book about Mardale 'A Backwater in Lakeland' by Isaac Hinchcliffe, was at one time the only book written entirely about the dale, and this was republished in recent years.

The beauty and atmosphere of the dale was chosen by Antony Trollope as the setting for his novel 'Can you forgive her?' Mrs Humphrey Ward included some locations in the Mardale area in her novel 'Robert Elsmere' and Hall Caine used the story of the runaway horse on the Corpse Road in 'Shadow of a Crime'. There have been many more books written about the dale since the 1930s; some are factual and historical whilst others are fictional. The valley has also been used as a film set, and even the location for a car advertising film.

Poets

Beautiful landscape and nostalgic memories of the community have inspired many poets to write about Mardale and Haweswater. Probably the earliest poem, if we can describe it as such, is Mardale Hunt, the song traditionally sung at the Mardale meets. The first verse is:

The morn is here, awake my lads,
Away! Away
The hounds are giving mouth, me lads,
Away! My lads Away!
The Mardale Hunt is out to-day,
Joe Bowman strong will lead the way,
Who ne'er has led his hunt astray,
Away! My lads Away!

It continues:

When darkness come to Mardale, hie
Away! Away!
For who the Dun Bull dares defy?
Away! My lads, Away!
Hal Usher kind will find a bed,
To rest our limbs, and lay our head,
We're welcomed, housed, and warmed and fed,
Away!, My lads, Away!

In winter Mardale's dree and drear,
Away! Away!
But 'tis not so if the Hunt is here,
Away! My lads, Away!
We trencher well, we trencher long,
We meet in drink, we meet in song,
For days are short and nights are long,
Away, My lads, Away!

William Wordsworth was familiar with Haweswater; in his poem 'The Brothers', he uses part of Kidstow Pike as inspiration.

Aye, there indeed, your memory is a friend
That does not play you false. On that tall pike,
(It is the loneliest place of all these hills)
There were two Springs which bubbled side by side, *
As if they had been made that they might be
Companions for each other: ten years back,
Close to those brother fountains, the huge crag
Was rent with lightning—one is dead and gone,
The other, left behind, is flowing still.

(*Note on the line *'There were two springs which bubbled side by side.'* The impressive circumstance here described actually took place some years ago in this country, upon an eminence called Kidstow Pike, one of the highest of the mountains that surround Hawes-water. The summit of the pike was stricken by lightning; and every trace of one of the fountains disappeared, while the other continued to flow as before.) Kidstow Pike is obviously Wordsworth's spelling of Kidsty Pike.

Wordsworth also uses a memorial stone in Mardale churchyard as inspiration for part of 'The Excursion'. He notes:

'Then that of the deaf man, whose epitaph may be seen in the churchyard at the head of Haweswater, and whose qualities of mind and heart, and their benign influence in conjunction with his privation, I had from his relatives on the spot.'

The inscription may still be seen on one of two copper plates attached to a sandstone memorial which is now in the Mardale Burial Ground area of Shap churchyard.

Here lieth Thomas Holme son of the late Henry and Jane Holme of Chapel Hill.

He was deprived of the sense of hearing in his youth and lived about 50 years without the comfort of hearing one word.

He reconciled himself to his misfortune by reading, and useful employment.

He was very temperate, honest and peaceable.

He was well respected by his neighbours and relations and departed this life after a short sickness on 22nd March 1773 aged 67 years.

Here is an extract from the poem:

The Excursion - Book Seventh - Churchyard among the mountains

Traced faintly in the greensward; there, beneath
A plain blue stone, a gentle Dalesman lies,
From whom, in early childhood, was withdrawn
The precious gift of hearing. He grew up
From year to year in loneliness of soul;
And this deep mountain-valley was to him
Soundless, with all its streams. The bird of dawn
Did never rouse this Cottager from sleep
With startling summons; not for his delight
The vernal cuckoo shouted; not for him
Murmured the labouring bee. When stormy winds
Were working the broad bosom of the lake
Into a thousand thousand sparkling waves,
Rocking the trees, or driving cloud on cloud
Along the sharp edge of yon lofty crags,
The agitated scene before his eye
Was silent as a picture: evermore

In his 'Guide to the Lakes', Wordsworth describes Haweswater as:

'... a little Ullswater with the advantage that it remains undefiled by the intrusion of bad taste.'

Thomas Watson of Fellgate near Renwick was a mason by trade and also one of the first adherents of Wesley on the fellside, having been taken as a boy to hear John Wesley preach at Gamblesby. He was a man of broad and liberal views and although uneducated, he never failed to make a pleasing rhyme describing the people and places he had visited. He was a favourite of local gentry, often visiting Nawarth, and Greystoke Castles, Edenhall, Patterdale Hall, Staffield House, Newbiggin Hall, the College at Kirkoswald and others. He could barely write so he committed his verse to memory, many of his poems being composed when he was over 80 years old. Some of his friends decided to publish some of his poetry so they went to his house and wrote the poems down as the author dictated them; they are composed mainly in rough English. He died at the age of 90. This book of poetry, 'The Patriarch's Æolian Harp' was published by Herald Co Ltd, Penrith in 1906.

His poem 'Journey to Mardale' is perhaps not the best of poetry, but it conveys the nature of the dale. Here are a few verses:

When I went up to Mardale the journey was far,
The people were few and the children looked scar,
The dale it was long and in some places wide,
And there were high mountains on every side.

There aren't many houses – to give a call I didn't fail –
The last place I came to is called Rigging Dale –
A place so remote it laid off at the side,
And this is the place where the dale is so wide.

At Mr Holme's I hope you will find
That there is refreshment, and all that is kind,
And further than this it is pleasing to tell,
His mistress and children were looking so well.

Members of the Baily family wrote numerous poems whilst spending their holidays in the dale. The poems often describe the natural charm of the valley whilst others refer to people and events. A 'Saga of Mardale' praises all the charms of the dale and mentions several of the inhabitants and their attributes. This work is unsigned, so we do not know which member of the family wrote it:

'Tis Mardale the beauteous its saga I sing.
Land of the fir trees
Land of the snow-flecks,
On bare hillside lying
Dale of Haweswater
'Tis Mardale the Beauteous
Whose saga I sing.

Sheep on the fellside
Lads in the homesteads
Dale of the hardy
Dale for the simple
Such glory is thee
Great Mardale the Beauteous
Whose saga I sing.
Dwellers in Mardale
Your saga I sing.

Daffurn the trim one,
Barham the Pastor,
Forster the school dame,
Permanent dwellers
In Mardale the Beauteous
Whose saga I sing.

Greenhow the shepherd
With Violet his wench
His mistress the washer
And baker of bread
Long may you dwell here
In Mardale the beauteous
Whose saga I sing.

Hail son of Simp
And tall sons of thee
Kindly to small boys
Friendly to housewives
Thy mistress is she.
Dweller at Chapel Hill
Farm of Great Mardale
Whose saga I sing.

Bailys the numerous
Garston the strenuous
Host of great kindness
And bringers of great joy
To those of less lands
Return you for ever

To Mardale the Beauteous
Whose saga I sing.

All lovers of beauty
Join in the chorus
O Mardale the wondrous
Thy saga I sing.

Without doubt the natural beauty of the Haweswater valley and its surroundings has inspired many people to compose verse; they range from the works of famous poets to simple poems written anonymously. The valley is still a source of inspiration and its demise brought a new aspect to the poetry. Over the past seventy five years many have been moved to compose poems full of nostalgia and lament for what is now lost.

Jacob Thompson – The Height of Ambition

Jacob Thompson – The Downfall of Pride

Bowderthwaite Bridge – Helena Baily

Epilogue

When a little girl turned a key in the door of the Dun Bull on Monday 24th May 1936, locking it forever, she was not just closing a door on her own young life, but on the ancient lives of the generations who had populated Mardale. Countless families had lived and farmed Mardale's green fields, wooded uplands and high fells and cast their nets and rods into its lake and high tarns and forces. They had hewn lead and copper ores from its black earth and grey slates from its quarries for the roofs of their homes, and peat turfs from its high bogs to warm their houses, sported on High Street and worshipped in Mardale's little church.

The Holmes and the Edmondsons, the Baxters and the Hodgsons and many other families had issued forth from the farms that made up the small Mardale community - Chapel Hill, Grove Brae, Flakehow, Riggindale, Bowderthwaite, Brackenhowe, Sandhill, Measand, Colby and of course the dale's hostelry, the Dun Bull which had its own small farm.

In 1935 many of these farming families moved to carry on their living farther afield, but some remained in Cumberland and Westmorland. The Kitchings of Measand Beck Farm moved a little way down the valley to Naddle Farm which is still a large sheep farm to this day. John Lancaster of Flakehow departed for Hesket-Newmarket, while his near neighbour in Mardale, Tom Bell of Grove Brae, carried on his farming in Heltondale.[1]

Bob Daffurn, mine host at the Dun Bull and originally a Wiltshire man, continued to ply his trade in Westmorland at the Greyhound Inn in Shap.

In October 1935 the earthly remains of many families - the Holmes, some Bowsteads and Jacksons together with the Reverend Thomas Wharton who died in 1854 - were disinterred and transported to the new Mardale Cemetery at Shap. In November 1935 many Greenhows, Sarjeants and the Reverend Richard Hebson, who died in 1799, joined them.

People and places, a litany of memories echoing down through the annals of time, vivid in the minds of people living

Moving livestock

now. In sad times many of these families would previously have gathered by the foot of Hopgill Beck to accompany the remains of a deceased family member or friend (the coffin lashed securely to the back of a stout fell pony) by the corpse road that twisted and turned up the rough track, zig-zagging precariously until it reached the peat cotes near its top and then levelling off as the track crossed the even ground before it plunged down into Swindale and then on to Tailbert, Keld, and finally to the final burial place, St Michael's Church at Shap. The folk of Mardale must have been relieved when Mardale

New Mardale Cemetery at Shap

Church got its own consecrated ground in 1737.

Happier times ruled when sporting days took place on High Street (the Roman Road) and Shepherds Meets were held at the Dun Bull or fox hunts set off from there.

Harvest Festivals were joyous occasions as the years' toil was shown to have been fruitful, or perhaps sometimes not, the vagaries of fell farming proving not to be always kind. No doubt the hardy fell folk would have adapted and survived, for survivors they were.

Hard work, snow and rain, flood and drought they could endure but not the far reaching demands of Cottonoppolis (a word used by George Saintsbury to describe the cotton trade and the demands imposed by it on the workforces of the textile manufacturing towns of Lancashire and their farther environs).[(2)]

By 1831 Manchester's population had increased by nearly six times in sixty years; the greatest decennial rate of growth in the nineteenth century.[(3)] From a population of 90,000 in 1801 it had risen to 543,900 in 1901 and a startling 730,000 in 1921.[(4)] The strain on natural resources can only be imagined.

One only has to read Frederick Engels' vivid descriptions of the terrible conditions endured by the textile workers of Manchester to understand how the immediate resources of the region could not begin to supply the burgeoning population and industry in the twentieth century.(4)

Now, soon, very soon, Mardale would be filled with a leaden grey body of water; the lichened grey field walls and buildings drowned, tumbled by forces unleashed by the industrial revolution of the eighteenth century. The church, the last building in the dale to be demolished, left some small parts of its body in Mardale; the pews now shelter within the hollow buttress walls of the dam, their patina of years shaded by the reservoir dam walls that entombed them. Mardale Church's small, bright, stained glass windows now look out onto the reservoir from the draw down tower some 500 metres south of the hotel. The tower itself was partially built with stone from Mardale's Church.(5)

Mardale Church's weather vane (The Lamb of God) now butts its head into the winds above St Michael's at Shap; the communion plate from Mardale Church is also in St Michael's Church.(6)

No more would men wipe the sweat from their brows after a long day in the fields as they trod the path toward their homes and a well earned drink, and their wives and families rested from their labours in their farmsteads.

The growing mill towns of Lancashire and their industrial needs in the first decades of the twentieth century asked serious questions of the great northern watersheds. Greedy for more and yet more water to slake the thirsts of their expanding industries and growing workforces, Manchester asked and Mardale, reluctantly, gave.

Plaque to the memory of Hugh Parker Holme, St Michael's Church, Shap

A Prophecy

'What will Mardale be in the year 1954? In the past is has escaped, for good or evil, two possibilities – a tunnel through Gatescarth with a railway down the valley to Bampton and an experience like to Thirlmere's, which would have raised the water for Manchester to the very gate of the chapel. Would we rather see these intrusions on our ancestral simplicity or lapse like Swindale into an uninhabited solitude? But these things are in the womb of the future. Perhaps it is best not curiously to prognosticate, but to be thankful that we have known the chapelry as she was and is. What she is she will cease to be. Only the amphitheatre of mountains, silent spectators of the fluctuating fortunes of farmers and their flocks will without change guard the sweet vale of Haweswater to the end of time.'

Joseph Whiteside writing in 'Shappe in Bygone Days', 1904

Riggindale Bay and Wood Howe Island during the 1995 drought

Mardale Folk

The tale of Mardale is now complete
Of hunting days and shepherds meet
Of pig butching and all that tripe
And the postman falling off his bike.

Ike Cookson with his greetings warmly
Tot Greenhow on his trusty pony
The shepherds and their corny jokes
Are what made Mardale and its folks.

At the boathouse Earls went to play
With the 'Kings of Mardale' in their day
And stones long lost because of moss
Perhaps the base of Anna's Cross.

The quaint old church amongst the yews
Which he parson from a distance viewed
Or hurried homeward in the dark
Aware of the ghost at Rowan Park.

The school where kids did work and play
And dancers danced the night away
Where Miss Forster ruled, firm but fair
And taught with an artistic flair.

At Sandhills, on a craggy hill
The two Miss Kitchings showed their skill
Good plain food was their special theme
And at bed and breakfast reigned supreme.

The Dun Bull came in very handy
For a cosy chat or double brandy
Both despatched without remorse
By Daffurn in his neat plus fours.

At Flakehow, Mrs Jack Lancaster
Previewed the valley's worst disaster
Protest she knew would do no god
When fathoms deep beneath the flood.

You could roam the valley floor at will
From Measand Falls to chapel Hill
Or view it with shaded brow
From Lumley's Tower on Woody How.

And through the valley's total length
You'd find good men of wit and strength
To help their neighbours was their way
Be it clipping sheep or making hay.

On a bright and frost autumn morn
They would hear the sound of the hunting horn
And on hearing this would turn their feet
Towards the famous shepherds meet.

The huntsman's call rang loud and clear
'Cos hunties' name was 'Owd Joe Weir'
Who'd spent years in hunting gills and dells
And hours tramping Mardale fells.

Good shepherds trudged from off the ways
To perhaps return or claim their strays
Then sheep exchanged and light growing dull
Would refresh themselves at the old Dun Bull.

On greeting friends not often seen
Would use the phrase 'Hoo hes't been'
Then revel in a day well spent
And pass the night in merriment.

The Baily family's hearts desire
Was to enjoy their days at old Goosemire
But on this quest they did sometimes fail
And had to be content with Riggindale.

Being a farmer's wife was no mean feat
With long hours worked from morn till neet
No modern tools to help with chores
Like baking bread and cleaning floors.

Washdays were hardly days of fun
Having risen long before the sun
Of equipment there was no new fangle
Just arm aching hours at the mangle.

The landlord with his neat plus fours
The parson with his ancient clothes
The schoolmarm with her yen for dictation
The boatman with his fair complexion.

The shepherd tending to his flock
The farmer solid as a rock
All seen sometimes in different yolks
But that's what made those 'Mardale folks'.

All these scenes are now long gone
But still recalled in verse and song
And the 'Folks' are free from life's affray
May they rest in peace where ere they lay.

John Graham

Notes and Bibliography

Introduction

1. **Bradley, A G,** 1924 *Highways and Byways in the Lake District,* Macmillan and Co London
2. **Royal Commission on Historic Monuments of England,**1935, *Mardale*
3. **Wainwright, A,** 1957, *A Pictorial Guide to the Lakeland Fells, Book 2, the Far Eastern Fells,* Westmorland Gazette

Bibliography

Brabant, F G, 1952, *The English Lakes,* Methuen and Co. Ltd, London

Bulmer, 1906, *History and Directory of Westmorland*

Hindle, B P, 1984, *Roads and Trackways of the Lake District,* Moorland Publishing.

Natural England, 1986, *SSSI schedule for Naddle Forest.*

Skipsey, Eric, 2004, *Geology,* article written for Mardale exhibition, collection at Shap Heritage Centre

Smith, Alan, 2008, *The Landscapes of Cumbria no 3, The Ice Age in the Lake District,* Rigg Side Publications

www.english-lakes.com

www.unitedutilities.com/haweswater estate

Chapter 1 Early Settlers

1. **Noble, Mary E,** 1901, *A History of the Parish of Bampton,* p 15, Titus Wilson, Kendal
2. **Noble, Mary E,** 1901, *A History of the Parish of Bampton,* p 16, Titus Wilson, Kendal

Bibliography

Bell, T, C, *Penrith's Roman Heritage,* Roman Survey Publications

Brennand, Mark (editor), 2006, *An Archaeological Research Framework for N.W. England (Vol 1),* The Association for Local Government Archaeology Officers & English Heritage with the Council for British Archaeology NW

Collingwood, W G and R G, editors, Transactions of the Cumberland and Westmorland Antiquarian & Archaeological Society, 1923, vol XX111 New Series, *Whelter Shielings,* Titus Wilson, Kendal

Collingwood, W G and Collingwood, R G, Transactions of the Cumberland and Westmorland Antiquarian & Archaeological Society, 1923, Vol 23, pp285-6. *Castle Crag*

Cross, Nigel, *The Celts, Pastoral Farming and domestic animals,* ww.resourcesforhistory.com

English Heritage, National Monuments Record, Monument Report UI 11065. *Shielings 10th, 11th*

Fell, Clare, 1972, *Early Settlement in the Lake Counties,* Dalesman Publishing

Pearsall, W H, Pennington, W, 1973, *The Lake District: a Landscape History*, Collins

Royal Commission on Historical Monuments of England: Westmorland 1936, His Majesty's Stationery Office

Scott, Joe (editor), 1995, *A Lakeland Valley through Time: A History of Stavely, Kentmere and Ings*, Staveley and District History Society

Waterhouse, John 1985, *The Stone Circles of Cumbria*, Camelot Press

Whaley, Diana, 2006, *A Dictionary of Lake District Place Names*, English Place Name Society, Nottingham

Chapter 2 The Manor of Thornthwaite

1. **Carlisle Record Office:** D/Lons/L5/4/30/16 *Stone and slate repairs*
2. **Carlisle Record Office:** D/Lons/L5/2/20/12 *Rook rent Measand*
3. **Nicholson, J and R Burn,** *The History and Antiquities of the Counties of Westmorland and Cumberland*, Vol 1, p 292-4, *Pout hens*
4. **Carlisle Record Office:** D/Lons/L5/4/30/16 *Boon days 1782*
5. **Carlisle Record Office:** D/Lons/L5/2/20/5 *Thomas Mounsey*
6. **Carlisle Record Office:** D/Lons/L5/2/20/5 *Tenants call book*
7. **Carlisle Record Office:** *Fishing licence 1726*
8. **Carlisle Record Office:** D/Lons/L5/1/35/4 *Quarries Lease*
9. **Kendal Record Office:** WPR/84 *Overseers Accounts; Apprenticeships*
10. **Carlisle Record Office:** D/Lons/L5/4 Thornthwaite Box 1, File 3 *Wharling, chimney, glass*
11. **Carlisle Record Office:** D/Lons/L5/4 Thornthwaite Box 1, File 3, *Naddle Receipts*
12. **Carlisle Record Office:** D/Lons/L5/4 Box 1, File 3, *Lord Jimmy, wood*
13. **Carlisle Record Office:** D/Lons/L5/2/20/14 *Rebuild walls*
14. **Bouch and Jones,** *Curwen tenants, Thornthwaite Hall 1576*

Bibliography

Carlisle Record Office: Miscellaneous papers from D/Lons/L5

Curwen, John F, 1932, *The Later Records relating to North Westmorland*, Titus Wilson, Kendal

Curwen, John F, 1928, *History of the House of Curwen*, Titus Wilson, Kendal

Nicolson, J and Burn, R, *The History and Antiquities of the Counties of Westmorland and Cumberland*, Vol 1

Noble, Mary E, 1901, *A History of the Parish of Bampton*, Titus Wilson, Kendal

Parson, Wm, and White, Wm, 1829, History, *Directory and Gazetteer of Cumberland and Westmorland*, repub. Michael Moon

Chapter 3 Traditional Life, Customs and Legends

1. **Whiteside, Joseph,** *Shappe in Bygone Days, p118*, Titus Wilson, Kendal
2. **Garston, Gwendolen,** *Goosemire Guardian*, unpublished family newspaper compiled by the Baily family (Private collection)

3. **Collingwood, W G,** *An Inventory of the Ancient Monuments of Wesmorland and Lancashire-North-of-the Sands,* CWAAS Transactions XXVI New series
4. Agreement between Edward Hassell and Messrs Walker, Ion, Robinson and Walter to produce charcoal. (Unpublished, January 1749) Dalemain Archive
5. Recording of Tom Edmondson made by Jean Scott Smith (1977) (Private collection)
6. *Wilson's Shepherds Guide* ,1913, Lancaster, Brash, Eaton and Bullfield
7. *A Travelling Actress in the North and Scotland – Memoirs of the Life of Mrs Charlotte Deans 1768-1859,* 1837, Wigton

Bibliography

Dickinson, William, 1875, *Cumbriana, or Fragments of Cumbrian Life,* Callander & Dixon, Whitehaven

Noble, Mary E, 1901, *History of the Parish of Bampton,* Titus Wilson, Kendal

Chapter 4 Mardale Homesteads

1. **Royal Commission on Historic Monuments of England,** 1935, Survey of Mardale
2. **Gwendolen Garston,** August 1924, *Goosemire Guardian*
3. **Radcliffe, Ann,** 1795, *A journey made in 1794, through Holland and the frontier of Germany, with a return down the Rhine; to which are added observations during a tour of the lakes of Lancashire, Westmorland and Cumberland.*
4. **Hay, David and Joan,** 1976, *Mardale the drowned village,* Friends of the Lake District
5. **Baily, K, O,** *Riggindale Record,*
6. **Baily, Helena,** *Riggindale Record,* c.1930
7. **Baily, Helena,** *Riggindale Record,* c.1930

Chapter 5 Mardale Chapel

1. **Whiteside, Joseph,** 1904, *Shappe in Bygone Days, p100,* Titus Wilson, Kendal
2. **Whiteside, Joseph,** 1904, *Shappe in Bygone Days,* p99, Titus Wilson, Kendal
3. **Whiteside, Joseph,** 1904, *Shappe in Bygone Days,* p96, Titus Wilson, Kendal
4. **Whiteside, Joseph,** 1904, *Shappe in Bygone Days* p99, Titus Wilson, Kendal
5. **Hinchcliffe, I,** 1st pub 1925, 2Ravens edition pub 2001, *A Backwater in Lakeland*
6. **Royal Commission on the Historic Monuments of England,** 1935
7. **Whiteside, Joseph,** 1904, *Shappe in Bygone Days* p92, Titus Wilson, Kendal
8. **Whiteside, Joseph,** 1904, *Shappe in Bygone Days* p105, Titus Wilson, Kendal

9. **Ruridecanal Magazine,** extracts collected by Miss Jane Forster, archive held by John Graham
10. Collection of newspaper cuttings, Fairer Archive, held at Shap Heritage Centre
11. **Ruridecanal Magazine**
12. **Ruridecanal Magazine**
13. Helena Baily's memoirs from a tape recording made in 1995

Bibliography

Collingwood, W, G, 1949 edition, *The Lake Counties,* J M Dent and Sons, London

Noble, Mary E, 1901, *History of the Parish of Bampton,* Titus Wilson, Kendal

Parish Registers of Shap and Bampton

Chapter 6 The Dun Bull

1. **Noble, Mary,** 1901, *History of Bampton, Kidsty Pike by Bowman 1772,*Titus Wilson, Kendal
2. **Westmorland Gazette** *25th April 1840*
3. **Visitor's Book,** The Dun Bull, Fishwick family, private collection
4. **Whiteside, Joseph,** 1904, *Shappe in Bygone Days,* Titus Wilson, Kendal
5. **Rawnsley, H, D,** 1906, *Months at the Lakes, November, The Mardale Shepherds Meeting,* James MacLehose and Sons, Glasgow
6. **Whiteside, Joseph,** 1904, *Shappe in Bygone Days,* p81, Titus Wilson, Kendal

Bibliography

Graham, John, 2006-2010, Recollections of Mardale, in conversations with Jean Jackson

Logan Thompson, Bruce, 1942, *Mardale and Haweswater*

Chapter 7 The Schools

1. **Noble, Mary**, 1901, *The History of the Parish of Bampton, p132,* Titus Wilson, Kendal
2. **Noble, Mary**, 1901, *The History of the Parish of Bampton, pp128-130,* Titus Wilson, Kendal
3. **Parson and White**, 1829, *History, Directory and Gazetteer of Westmorland*
4. **Forster, Jane,** School entries for 1897, *School records,* unpublished private collection
5. **Forster, Jane** *Scrapbook, compiled from the Ruridecanal Magazine,* unpublished private collection, covers the years 1896-1933

Chapter 8 Wills and Inventories of some Mardale Families

Original copies Records of Wills and Inventories, Cumbria Record Office, Carlisle.

Transcription by Shap Local History Society

Chapter 9 The Kings of Mardale
1. **Whiteside, Joseph,** 1904, *Shappe in Bygone Days,* p107, Titus Wilson, Kendal
2. **Whiteside, Joseph,** 1904, *Shappe in Bygone Days* p110, Titus Wilson, Kendal
3. **Ruridecanal Magazine,** extracts collected by Miss Jane Forster, archive held by John Graham
4. Information from the Green family papers
5. **Whiteside, Joseph,** *In and around Mardale,* collection of newspaper cuttings from the Cumberland and Westmorland Herald 1935-6, Fairer archive held at Shap Heritage Centre

Chapter 10 Days of Exploration and Adventure
1. **Hay, David and Joan,** 1976, *Mardale the drowned village,* Friends of the Lake District
2. **Hinchcliffe, I,** 1st pub 1925, 2Ravens edition pub 2001, *A Backwater in Lakeland*

Extracts from Mardale Mercury, Goosemire Guardian, Riggindale Record - Baily family private collection

Helena Baily - from a tape recording made August 1995 at Shap, and her memoirs written shortly afterwards.

Chapter 11 Artists, Poets and Writers
1. **Heaton Cooper, Alfred,** 2006, *The English Lakes, Memories of the Past.*
2. **Otley, Jonathan,** 1850, *Guide to the English Lakes and adjacent mountains,* Otley
3. **Holt, David,** *David Holt's Victorian Walks: A three day's ramble in the Lake District in the Spring of 1856, Shap to Windermere*

Bibliography

Bradley, A G, 1924, *Highways and Byways in the Lake District,* Macmillan

Jewitt, Llewellyn, 1822, *Life, the biography of Jacob Thompson*

Epilogue
1. Personal conversation with John Metcalfe of Sunset View, Bomby, Bampton, Cumbria.
2. **Briggs, Asa** , 1968, *Victorian Cities:* p 96, 98, Penguin Books
3. **Briggs, Asa,** 1968. *Victorian Cities:* p 89, Penguin Books
4. **Engels, Frederick,** 1892, *Condition of the Working Class in England in 1844*: 42-74, Swan Sonnenschein & Co
5. **Berry, Geoffrey,** 1984, *Mardale Revisited*: p 84
6. Church Pamphlet, 1995, *Memories of Mardale,* St Michael's Church, Shap

Further reading

The story of the building of the dam is covered in *Cast Iron Community – The Story of Burnbanks,* 2006, Bampton and District History Society.

Mardale is also mentioned in the following books. Unless stated these are all in the library at Shap Heritage Centre.

Bampton and District History Society, 2003, *Ploughing in Latin,* Bookcase, Carlisle
Brabant, F G, 1952, *The Little guides: The English Lakes,* Methuen and Co (Private collection)
Bradley, A, G, 1901, *Highways and Byways of the Lake District,* Macmillan and Co
Emmett, Charlie, 1985, *In Search of Westmorland,* Cicerone Press (Private collection)
Ferguson, 1894, *A History of Westmorland*
Ffinch, Michael, 1985, *Penrith and the East Fellside,* Hale
Griffin, A, H, 1966, *Pageant of Lakeland,* Hale
Haswell, Frances (transcribed by), 1898, *The Register Book of Mardale Chappel*
Hindle, Brian P, 1984, *Roads and Trackways of the Lake District,* Moorland Publishing (Private collection)
Hodgson, H W, 1968, *A Bibliography of Cumberland and Westmorland*
Jones, Sir Clement, 1955, *Walks in North Westmorland,* Titus Wilson, Kendal (Private collection)
Lofthouse, J, 1976, *The Curious Traveller through Lakeland,* Hale
Lofthouse, J, 1965, *Country Goers North,* Hale
Lofthouse, J, 1953, *Lancashire Westmorland Highway* ,Hale
Marsh, John, 1992, *The Westmorland Lakes in Old Photos,* Alan Sutton
Mee, Arthur (editor), 1937, *The Lake Counties,* Hodder and Stoughton (Private collection)
Mitchell, W, R, 1966, *Men of Lakeland,* Phoenix House, London
Moseley, F, (editor), 1978, *The Geology of the Lake District,* Yorkshire Geological Society
Nicolson, N, 1969, *Greater Lakeland*
Nicolson, N, 1972, *Portrait of the Lakes*
Palmer, William T, 1946, *More Odd Corners in Lakeland,* Skeffington and Son (Private collection)
Parker, J, 1976, *Cumbria, A guide to the Lake District*
Pearsall, W, H and Pennington, W, 1977, *The Lake Distric* , Collins
Pevsner, N, *Buildings of England: Cumberland and Westmorland*
Rollinson, W, 1978, *A History of Cumberland and Westmorland,* Phillimore
Smith, K, 1973, *Cumbrian Villages*
Thompson, B, L, 1942, *Transactions of the Cumberland and Westmorland Antiquarian and Archaeological Society, Vol XLII*
Wainwright, A, *Old Roads of Eastern Lakeland,* Westmorland Gazette (Private collection)
Williams, L, A, 1975, *Road Transport in Cumbria in the 19th century,* George Allan and Unwin (Private collection)

Index